Work Experience Manual and Resource Action Kit

GILL SHARP and RUTH SHIEFF

KOGAN
PAGE

First published in 1991

Kogan Page Limited
120 Pentonville Road
London N1 9JN

© Gillian Sharp and Ruth Shieff, 1991

British Library Cataloguing in Publication Data

A CIP record for this book is available from the British Library.

ISBN 0 7494 0439 6

Typeset by DP Photosetting, Aylesbury, Bucks
Printed and bound in Great Britain
by Biddles Ltd, Guildford

Contents

List of Chapter Appendices, Tables and Figures

Monitoring

Debriefing

Special Issues

How to Use this Book

The Work Experience Manual takes you step-by-step through the process of setting up maintaining and concluding a work experience placement. We have supplied you with nearly every form, letter and checklist you might need along the way to cope with parents, employers and the students themselves. This material you will find either in the form of Appendices at the end of each chapter (signposted in the text) or as figures in the text; page references to both are detailed in the List of Chapter Appendices, Tables and Figures on pages 7–8. Following the last chapter on Special Issues you will find a further three Appendices. The first provides case study material which may be useful in outlining the kinds of problems likely to arise during work experience, and the second and third focus on legislation relevant to the area.

Introduction

Work experience was first introduced into the school curriculum by the 1973 Education (Work Experience) Act which – coming hot on the heels of the raising of the school leaving age – enabled schools for the first time to offer pupils in their last year of their compulsory education, the opportunity to spend some time gaining practical experience of the workplace – as part of an educational programme.

It has come a long way since those early days when it was sometimes viewed as a good way of getting rid of recalcitrant pupils who were disinclined to more academic pursuits. Nowadays, as its educational merits have become fully recognised, work experience is widely viewed as a standard curriculum entitlement for year 10 or 11 pupils across the full academic range. With TVEI now firmly established and the TVEE well under way, work experience remains centre stage. The National Curriculum makes economic and industrial understanding a 'cross-curricular theme', and work experience provides an excellent vehicle for ensuring that this element of the National Curriculum requirement is met. The National Curriculum requirement will provide further impetus for ensuring that work experience is fully integrated into all curriculum areas. Furthermore, as more and more schools become involved in Compacts, where the successful completion of a two-week work experience placement is one of the five specified goals, the pressure on schools to deliver work experience programmes is tremendous.

Work experience has long been part of many vocational courses in further education, for example Nursery Nurse Examination Board (NNEB) courses. However, the concept of work experience as introduced by the 1973 Act has had its impact in this area too. A three-week work experience placement (generally specified more broadly as '15 days' to allow for greater flexibility in arrangements) has become a requirement for most vocational courses run in further education (CPVE, BTEC etc). The distinction between the 'training placement' concept of many vocational courses, where the objectives were more clearly job specific, and the broad educational aims of work experience, has become blurred.

The trend towards including work experience in the curriculum has spread to take in many sixth-formers and those in colleges of further education, on more general academic courses. In this area an element of 'work shadowing' of professional or managerial type occupations, is often built into the experience.

In polytechnics too the concept of work experience is no longer confined to the traditional sandwich course arrangement. Polytechnics have been quick to integrate a period of work experience into a much fuller range of courses. The practice is now spreading to academic courses in all types of higher education institutions.

Add to this the number of Youth Training and Employment Training schemes in which work experience forms an integral part, and it is evident that work experience has been a growth area for the last 15 years.

As schools and colleges have become quickly aware of the volume of work and level of expertise involved in setting up and running quality work experience programmes, so the management and organisation of work experience programmes has become professionalised.

In very many areas, school-based work experience coordinators are supported by some form of centralised work experience coordination service. This may be in the form of a local education authority appointed work experience coordinator to serve the schools within that authority's area, or of a Compact work experience coordinator to serve Compact schools in their area. In other areas, the Careers Service or TVEI centre performs this centralised function. In other areas again, Project Trident acts in the same way.

The nature of the service these initiatives offer varies tremendously. Some initiatives see their primary function as developing and maintaining a central bank of employers sympathetic to approaches from schools for work experience. They may also be useful sources of advice and guidance, for example on matters of health and safety. Others may vet and approve placements on behalf of the authority. Others again take this central coordination a step further and may get involved in allocating placements to schools and institutions in their area, matching placements to students, or in the preparation and debriefing of students. Some centralised initiatives will undertake to find and confirm a proportion of the placements required, leaving the individual school to make up the shortfall. Others see their role strictly as a coordinating one, rationalising the use of resources and maintaining quality.

Within colleges of further education, these centralised functions are often performed by a college-based further education work experience coordinator whose relationship to individual course tutors often mirrors that of a local authority work experience coordinator's relationship to schools. The role they play will often be largely determined by the size of the college, and the range and number of courses offering work experience.

Clearly the level of support offered to the college course tutor, or to the school-based work experience coordinator is largely determined by the resources of the centralised function. There are, however, still many teachers and lecturers who have sole and total responsibility for all aspects of work experience in their school from setting up their own placement bank, through to staff training. Whatever the local arrangements may be, a substantial element of responsibility for all aspects of the planning, delivery and quality of work experience programmes remains in the hands of the individual school work experience coordinator, or the college course tutor.

WORK EXPERIENCE AND EUROPE

Yes it had to happen, the *entente cordiale* has been extended to work experience. Links with other European countries have tended to spring up informally in the past, often as the result of town twinning arrangements. More recently, enterprising teachers of specific courses, such as A level languages or bilingual secretarial studies, have made reciprocal arrangements with European counterparts. Sometimes only one course has been involved, often it has spread to take in whole institutions and in some cases, entire areas of the country – witness the Isle of Wight which has a flourishing work experience arrangement with several of its neighbours on the Continent.

Already there are signs that over the next few years commercial, educational and charitable agencies are going to become increasingly involved in the provision of placements in the EC – for teachers as well as students. However, when this happens and, whether centrally coordinated or not, all the suggestions and stratagems which we've made re locally based work experience will apply equally to its continental equivalent.

A range of publications is available from a variety of sources, which look at work experience in the curriculum, the philosophy of work experience, and so on. In addition to publications by academics, many TVEI, National Curriculum Council and SCIP publications also look at work experience together with related subjects – work shadowing, the work-related curriculum, economic and industrial awareness, the future of work experience and so on.

We hope that this book will complement existing publications in supplying a need for a step-by-step practical guide to work experience – one which is friendly in style, easy to read, and easy to access as a reference document.

We intend that the book will lay out in easy stages the whole process of running a work experience programme.

Samples of documentation and materials are also extensively provided in this book. These materials can be readily adapted to suit individual needs and we hope that they will enable teaching staff to see more clearly the whole process of work experience, gain an overview of what is involved, and that they will therefore provide the basic framework of a successful work experience scheme.

We have also included some case studies, role plays and anecdotes which we hope will bring the issues to life.

Finally a few words about the future of work experience.

Local management of schools will no doubt bring changes in the way in which work experience is funded. If schools are required to buy-in the services of a centralised work experience coordination service, this will of course mean that work experience will have to compete for resources with the other demands made on schools' budgets. TECs may well have a much more influential role to play in the funding arrangements as well as in the supply of work experience placements (through their close links with employers). Changes in the funding arrangements of the Careers Service and of colleges of further education may also provide a further stimulus for examining carefully the role of work experience in the curriculum. Demographic trends and economic factors are also having their impact on work experience programmes – causing many employers to reflect carefully on the cost implications of offering work experience, weighed against the longer-term benefits to their industry.

However, our observations and conversations lead us to the firm conviction that work experience has now solidly established its place as an integral part of education, and is here to stay.

From their differing perspectives all the parties involved (pupils, students, parents, teachers and employers) view work experience as a worthwhile and exciting opportunity. We believe that work experience is firmly established in the curriculum, indeed it is the initiative out of which a whole host of other kinds of education-industry collaboration has developed and flourished. It has made educationalists aware of the tremendous resource which exists among employers, and has made employers more aware of the challenges faced by educationalists and the important contribution they can make to facing those challenges.

We hope that this book will provide practical advice and information which will enable you to approach the planning, managing and resourcing of your work experience programme with confidence and enthusiasm.

1
Objectives

This first chapter looks at goals; setting them, prioritising them, and communicating them to others – three important steps. Being clear on your goals and ensuring that they are shared by all parties is the foundation stone for the success of work experience. The major causes of the breakdown of placements are conflicting perceptions of the objectives of the placement, differing priorities, and the failure of the organiser to communicate her/his goals and ensure that they are shared by others involved.

SETTING YOUR OBJECTIVES

The range of possible objectives for work experience is wide, and will vary from student to student, year group to year group, course to course. Of all possible objectives, not all will be appropriate for all students. You will need to decide not only which are valid for your students, but also the relative priority you wish to give each of your goals. Some goals are fairly central: 'life and social skills' and 'broad vocational awareness' (see page 16) are likely to be appropriate to some degree for virtually all students. Indeed for some students they will be the exclusive goals. Other objectives may also be valid but perhaps less central.

Having set your objectives and prioritised them, you will then need to ensure that all parties – employers, teachers, parents and students – have the same objectives as yourself. Conflicting perceptions of the objective of the placement and differing priorities are two of the major underlying causes of disappointment and ultimately of the breakdown of placements.

It can be surprisingly difficult to budge preconceptions about work experience. It may not even have occurred to any of the parties that there is any perception but their own, but there is a tendency to 'switch off' in the face of evidence 'which does not compute', as it were. But the importance of making objectives crystal clear and ensuring common understanding is paramount.

Say, for example, the pupils perceive job training or career sampling to be the primary objective of the placement. They may be disappointed by the lack of formal training received at their placement. Add to this the feelings of some parents, who perceive work experience as a kind of pre-employment trial period and therefore feel affronted and angry that the placements do not match the aspirations they have for their children.

Into the lethal brew of mixed perceptions add the employers, who may perhaps see the placement principally as an indirect method of recruitment. They then apply inappropriate selection criteria or expect a higher level of commitment than is realistic. Finally, add the last ingredient – the hapless teacher who perceives the placement as principally a 'life skills' exercise.

All the above perceptions of the objectives may have some validity, but will not necessarily be the sole or primary objective for every placement. Clearly then, it is not only the objectives themselves which must be made explicit, but the relative priorities of each.

With these points in mind, consider the appropriateness of the following list of possible objectives for work experience:

1   Life and social skills: work experience as a 'maturing agent'
- Working alongside adults as colleagues (rather than as parents, teachers, or figures of authority.
- Learning responsibility by being part of a team, eg that being late or absent for work leaves others with extra work, or the problem of rescheduling the day's work.
- Being away from school friends and standing on your own feet.
- Experiencing new environments, overcoming nerves,
- Making relationships, explaining to colleagues who you are, why you are there.
- Taking initiatives; seeing and learning what needs to be done and getting on with it without waiting to be asked; offering help.
- Dealing with problems, eg approaching a supervisor for help, asking for work.
- Gaining self-confidence.

2   Broad vocational awareness
Work experience might form part of a programme of study covering a range of work-related issues, eg:

- Trade unionism, staff associations and other methods of negotiation and communication,
- Women at work, childcare, sexual harassment, equal pay, sex stereotyping in jobs, and so on,
- Racial and religious issues on the workplace,
- Other equal opportunities issues – disability, age, sex,
- Organisational structures (partnerships, public sector organisations, cooperatives, limited companies, public liability companies, charities, etc).

3   Liberal/general education
For many students, the experience of a side of life to which they might otherwise never be exposed, can be intellectually stimulating, horizon-broadening, or even character building. This experience can produce a 'more rounded' personality with a fuller and more enriched appreciation of the world. Such experience can be presented – alongside academic achievement – as a positive personal asset, in applications to higher education or for jobs. For example, a placement in a day nursery, or a home for the handicapped or elderly, can raise social

awareness, responsibility, and an understanding of the issues to do with caring for others. This can be viewed as a useful preparation for life and citizenship for all students – not just for those who wish to enter the 'caring professions'. In fact it could be argued that such an experience would be especially appropriate for those planning a career in a field which would not normally expose them to this kind of social reality. Pupils from sheltered or deprived environments can, equally, gain useful insight, understanding, raised aspirations, self and social awareness and confidence from a well chosen placement.

4 Subject enhancement

Work experience can be used to make academic subjects more industry-related and, conversely, the world of work can be used to enrich school subjects. A placement in a legal firm with visits to court, police stations, and prison, can offer an interesting insight into one or more 'social institutions' and form the basis of a social science project. A placement in a museum or library can support and enrich a local history project. The drawing up of a curriculum vitae or writing a thank you letter can be part of English course work, and so on.

5 Task or job-specific training

Through work experience students may have the opportunity to learn to use a particular piece of equipment or technology or to acquire other job-specific skills – opportunities which are not available in school or cannot be simulated in the classroom. Some examples are:

- desk-top publishing;
- computer graphics;
- reception and telephone skills;
- car maintenance;
- running a small business.

6 Vocational preparation and acquisition of job-getting skills

Work experience affords the opportunity to acquire the informal information and familiarity with an industry which will enable the student to present her/himself more effectively for a job, eg:

- Making useful personal contacts. In many industries this is still important.
- Learning methods of entry, career routes, qualifications and qualities needed, from the people already in the industry. Often this advice – however unencouraging – is more readily accepted than the same advice from a careers adviser or teacher.
- Picking up informal information about careers – the jargon, the issues, the gossip, the trends.
- Getting an employer reference with respect to attitude, enthusiasm, acceptability. After a longer placement, employers may also be willing to give references relating to the ability to do the job.

7 Career sampling

It is a common misperception that career sampling is the main objective of work experience.

Only for a minority of 'vocationally mature' students, who have made committed and informed career choices, is this likely to be the case. Mature or adult students, who are following vocational courses in further or higher education, and who have had professional careers' guidance, might fall into this category. However, for most students career sampling as a goal will be peripheral, or indeed irrelevant. Furthermore, even for the 'vocationally committed' student, sampling or observing one job with one employer for a brief period carries the danger of giving a distorted, misleading, or unrepresentative impression of that career.

Career sampling, as a goal for work experience, *can* become valid, when a number of students sample different careers, with different employers, say, within a broad vocational area. They might each then report back on their experiences, in an organised and structured way, to others in their group, as part of a debriefing exercise.

Points, then, to consider when deciding on your objectives are:

- Are your students mature enough to have made informed, realistic career decisions? (Many 14/15-year-olds are still in the 'I want to be a racing driver' stage. So, come to that, are many 18-year-olds – nay, 40-year-olds.)
- Have your students received professional careers' advice?
- Does the student's careers' adviser support the student's choice?
- Have the students already opted for a career area? This might apply to students on vocational courses, though bear in mind that most vocational courses prepare students for a broad vocational area like 'office skills' or 'business and finance', rather than for a specific occupation. 'Business and finance' students might enter occupational fields as widely varying as health service administration, retail management, or hotel work, as well as those areas more commonly associated with 'business and finance', such as accountancy, banking and insurance.
- Are the students likely to remain in education and training for some time to come? If so then any career choice made at this stage, even a realistic and informed one, is likely to be transitory. Career choices made at age 16 by a student planning to remain in education, perhaps going on to higher education, must be viewed with caution.

Some common employer objectives

It is as well to be aware of some common employer objectives. A small minority of employers may be motivated by the misconception that work experience provides them with access to free labour. Most employers, however, know that two to three weeks (the average lengh of placement) is too short a time for a new employee, especially a young one, to become productive and able to work without supervision, even in the most routine of jobs. Any free labour the employer gets must be weighed against the time spent interviewing, 'inducting', supervising, supporting and 'debriefing' the student, and in briefing their existing staff. While some students are less demanding of time than others, most employers find that things balance themselves out in the long run; one student may work productively with little supervision, the next may need a good deal of time and patience.

So why, then, do they do it? Some common reasons are:

1   Promotion and public relations for the company, the product or the industry as a whole. (It can be almost a form of indirect advertising.):

- Raising awareness among the public of the company or product.
- Making a gesture of goodwill in order to maintain company reputation and good name.
- Educating and informing the public about their industry or profession.
- Dispelling stereotypes of their industry or profession.
- Improving recruitment long-term.

2 Improving the future labour market pool:

- Helping educationalists better prepare young people for work.
- Helping educationalists develop students for adult life and social responsibility.

3 Pre-employment trial period:

- Employers may hope that sooner or later they will have a student on work experience to whom they wish to offer a permanent job. In fact the timing of work experience on some vocational courses may be geared to this.

COMMUNICATING YOUR OBJECTIVES

Objectives, as we have seen, may vary from student to student, placement to placement, school to school, course to course, year group to year group.

However, setting the objectives is a relatively futile exercise *unless you communicate them effectively to all parties concerned*, so that all are working towards the same goals. This is essential in order to avoid (or at least minimise) the problems which can arise through false, unrealistic or conflicting expectations.

The parties concerned are:

- Students.
- Parents/guardians.
- Employers.
- Others in the workplace.
- The work experience coordinator.
- Teacher colleagues; those involved in the preparation, debriefing or visiting of students on placement.

Chapter 3 provides some samples of written materials (letters, etc) which can be used in the communication process.

Other ways of communicating your objectives are:

Students

- Meetings, assemblies, tutorial time.
- Course and class work.
- Visits by pupils to placement and workplaces.

Parents

- Parents' evenings.

- Encouraging colleagues to discuss work experience with parents at every opportunity, during parents' evenings and other discussions,
- Involvement of parents in placement finding.

Employers and others in the workplace

- Visits to the workplace by teacher prior to the placement.
- Attendance of teachers or work experience coordinator at in-company training or staff meetings.
- Organised, structured visits by employers and their staff to the school.

Teaching colleagues

- INSET.
- Assemblies.,
- Involvement of staff in placement finding (which can raise awareness of employers' needs).
- Staff meetings.
- Involvement of staff in preparation, visiting and debriefing.

2

Planning work experience and finding placements

Once you are certain of your aims and objectives, you need to consider what resources you will need and the 'hows' and 'wheres' of finding work experience.

The setting up of any work experience scheme requires careful planning, preparation and administration. Initially this may seem like a lot of unnecessary extra effort, especially if you are raring to go and you have a lot of good ideas which you want to put into practice. However, time and effort expended at this stage will pay dividends later, while a more haphazard approach can result in chaos, eg poor timing, lost or mislaid information, and an incipient nervous breakdown! If you want to avoid this fate, read on.

TIME SCALE

The amount of time needed to set up placements is often underestimated by new practitioners – and also, it must be said, by their line managers/heads of department/headteachers, etc. These latter sometimes fondly imagine that a mailshot, backed up by a few hours on the telephone, is all that is needed.

This is a fallacy. Last-minute or drastically curtailed arrangements *do* happen – and are often successful – but this is a case of the exception proving the rule.

Our suggested minimum timetable for a group of 15–20 students is 12 weeks – 12 months if you are sending out your whole fifth year of 150–200 pupils (see Table 2.1): this allows for all sorts of hitches as well as holidays, absence due to sickness and so forth.

Table 2.1 *Time chart*

Weeks (months) 1–3
Note number of students/type of placements needed.
Make initial enquiries/contacts.

Weeks (months) 4–7
Follow up the above with letters/phone calls/visits.

Weeks (months) 8–10
Allocate students to placements.
Students attend pre-placement visits/interviews.

Weeks (months) 11–12
Sort out last-minute changes.
Send out final details/confirmation letters.
Allocate staff to monitoring placements.

If you have plenty of employer contacts, you may be tempted to cut down on this allotment of time, but *beware!* Industry does not work to the same timetable as schools and colleges, so if you ring one of your 'tame' employers a month before work experience begins, any of the following could have happened:

1   He/she is on an annual skiing holiday for the next three weeks.
2   He/she would love to help, but the offices are due to be renovated and there will be no room for your student during this period.
3   He/she has moved to another department or left the company altogether and the new member of staff is not quite so forthcoming about last-minute placements.
4   As he/she had not heard from you, the placement has been offered to another school/college instead.

The golden rule is never to assume that contacts will be able to deliver the goods at the right time.
    Another common experience is that of obtaining an offer of one or more placements several months ahead of the projected date – quite usual if you are arranging work experience on a large scale. However firm you believe this offer to be, bear in mind that few employers are genuinely committed to a placement until they have received *written confirmation* and, preferably, a named student, complete with a CV and arrangements for a pre-placement interview. Employers are less likely to withdraw their offer of a placement if they feel that they are disappointing a named individual.
    At the very least, you should send a reply slip to the employer requesting confirmation of arrangements made to date and acceptance of the student to be allocated. All this may seem like a lot of additional effort, but it really does minimise the chances of a last-minute breakdown of your best laid plans.
    If you are asking some of your students to make their own arrangements (see Chapter 3),

allow the same time span, if not longer. Sometimes, especially with younger students, vague promises of placements do not materialise or a definite schedule is not set in motion.

RESOURCES NEEDED

Anyone organising work experience is necessarily going to be involved in a great deal of letter writing, making phone calls and administrative work. Find out, from the outset, which, if any, of the following resources will be available to you:

- Clerical help.
  If this is not forthcoming, you will have to allow for time to be spent on envelope filling, photocopying and similar routine yet vital tasks.
- Technical/secretarial support staff.
  Will you, for instance, be able to rely on the help of the reprographics technician (assuming one exists) at a moment's notice? If not, how much advance warning will be needed? If this help is not available, will you be able to use the local quick print shop?
- Will secretaries be willing and able to deal with messages and queries from employers?

It is also obvious that you will need:

1 Time
Placements cannot be cobbled together or conjured up out of a hat in a matter of days. Negotiate with your line boss the number of non-teaching hours which you might need (Table 2.1, the time chart, could be useful here too), depending on how much you need to organise.

If you are allocated what you consider to be insufficient time, emphasise this from the outset. That way, if things do go wrong, you will have covered yourself to a certain extent. If things go well, be sure to bask in the glory and to point out how it could be even better if you are given more time in the future!

2 Support from colleagues
This is essential. Some LEAs have full-time work experience coordinators who can provide help, information and advice. This is obviously a valuable source of support, although not one that can always be instantly on hand.

A word of warning, however: most of these work experience coordinators are well aware of the fragile and highly 'perishable' nature of the placements in their keeping. It is therefore highly unlikely that they will keep placements sitting on a shelf, as it were, waiting to be accessed by you. Most placements have an extremely short shelf-life, so a work experience coordinator who acts as a central resource will ensure that vacant places are passed as quickly as possible to the 'consumer'. This may be you or it may be another course or organisation which he/she is resourcing. Hence, any last-minute approach is likely to produce only suggested contacts, rather than 'hard' placements.

If you are lucky enough to have to have one of these beings operating in your area, your best bet is to involve them in your plans from the very beginning.

Whatever your outside circumstances, you will certainly need the backing of fellow staff in your own institution. For one thing, you will probably have to coopt them into helping with the preparation and monitoring of students. This can come as a nasty surprise to the uninitiated, so let them know what's going on at the outset. It can all be done quite simply and informally at staff/team meetings and you will find that colleagues may be able to provide helpful suggestions and ideas. They will certainly be more appreciative of all your hard work.

3   Facilities

In an ideal world, anyone coordinating a work experience scheme would have an office and a telephone line to themselves.

We appreciate that you are unlikely to be operating in such idyllic circumstances, but you will certainly need somewhere from which you can generate – and file – all the documentation needed. Hopefully, you will also have somewhere to make and receive phone calls in relative peace. If there is any way in which you can beg, steal or borrow an answerphone, we would warmly recommend it. It can circumvent major communication problems with employers.

Envisage the scene: an employer is trying to get in touch with you to discuss a possible placement. The phone line to the general office/staff room seems permanently engaged. When contact is finally established he/she is told that you are teaching and would they please call back during Period Five. This is frustrating for anybody, let alone an employer unaccustomed to the vagaries of the timetable. And remember, this is a sales market and you are the buyer. They've got it and you want it. Many employers will be deterred at an early stage if they have trouble contacting you. An answerphone may not be ideal, but at least both parties can keep in touch easily.

Possibly your school/college has a fax machine and this sort of situation is when it really comes into its own. A fax message is more immediate than an answerphone tape, it is quick to use and you can cover more points in greater detail. If you are lucky enough to have a fax, use it to the fullest extent.

Thus far we have only looked at the planning stages of work experience, but now you need to consider one other vital factor: timing.

TIMING OF WORK EXPERIENCE

From your point of view, you will want to have the work experience at a date which allows you sufficient time to prepare placements, employers and students.

You also have to allow for:

1   Legal considerations

The Work Experience Act 1973 was amended with effect from November 1990 to enable all school pupils to do work experience *from Easter of year 10*. Younger pupils must, by law, only watch (DES booklets, April 1991, *Work Experience: A Guide for Schools* and *Work Experience: A Guide for Employers*).

2   Exam dates and requirements

3   Other school/college activities

4 Holiday periods

Placements which start immediately after a vacation mean that last-minute hitches (and these do occur even with the most careful planning) may not be rectified in time. It is also important to give students their final briefing as near to the start of the placement as possible. Last-minute words of wisdom may be forgotten if a holiday intervenes. Similarly, placements which run into a holiday period carry the risk of minimising the effectiveness of the work experience. If students cannot give/receive feedback for three weeks or more, then the impact of the placement has often faded or been superseded by other events.

Given that the average term probably lasts for about three months, you may have little leeway for timing, particularly when you consider *placement availability*.

However, here are some pointers to take into account:

1 Employer's own situation

This is particularly important if you are dealing with a specific vocational course. For example, many financial organisations and departments will not take inexperienced students during their busy time, March and April, which is the end of the fiscal year. Other businesses, such as travel agencies and retail outlets also experience seasonal fluctuations in work.

Not all contingencies can be predicted in advance, however – witness the hapless work experience coordinator who tried to arrange a placement with a firm of stockbrokers the day after 'Black Monday'!

2 Off-peak periods

Many employers who are geared up to work experience actually bemoan the lack of takers during the late winter to early summer period. They may be oversubscribed in the summer and autumn, but between these dates many placements lie fallow.

3 Demand and supply

If you are operating in a small town, with only one or two schools and colleges, you have much more scope in terms of timing, although probably not in range of placements. In larger towns and cities, some firms are positively besieged by requests for work experience. In this case they may operate a 'first come, first served' policy or even a quota system. These are more good reasons for allowing a generous time scale: make sure that your requests get in ahead of those from neighbouring institutions. Remember that you are competing for placements with a whole plethora of agencies too – YT schemes, ET schemes and HE sandwich courses to name just a few.

4 The pecking order

Unless you have firm evidence that a longstanding employer contact will always give you 'first refusal', don't bank on having any priority.

Some organisations do fend off all comers with statements such as 'we have a longstanding commitment to St Oswald's students', but others are happy to work with several educational establishments.

Ultimately, placements are only ever 'owned' by the employer who offers them and they are the sole arbiter of who uses them.

When you have negotiated the timing of the work experience, you then have to turn your attention to how it will take place.

MODE OF ATTENDANCE

There are several possibilities: block placement, one/two days per week placement, and split placement. There are pros and cons to each.

Block placement

Pros

- Favoured by many employers.
- Easy to administer.
- Can enable specific tasks/projects to be undertaken.
- Offers an insight into the whole working week.
- Provides variety, continuity and the chance to build up relations at work.
- More chance to take on extra responsibilities and learn new skills.

Cons

Fairly inflexible: can be difficult to alter if the student or employer is unhappy.

One/two days per week

Pros

- Fits in well with certain courses (eg CPVE, NNEB).
- May allow student to become familiar with working life at a gentle pace.
- Easier for staff to visit.
- Some employers favour this as it means that they can put aside time to spend with the student.

Cons

- Some employers dislike it as being too disruptive to routine.
- Students may get a very narrow view of their work, ie if 'their' day is Tuesday they may never see processes carried out on a Friday.
- Some employers may save up specific (unpopular) tasks, eg filing, for this day.
- Tasks may need to be relearnt as students sometimes forget from week to week.
- Certain students find it easy to 'skive off'.

Split placement

This may involve a week one term, and two or more weeks the next.

Pros

- Provides a fairly gentle introduction to an industry.
- It is easy for alterations to be made/placements to be switched after the first week.

Cons

- Some students (and employers) give in to early difficulties in stage one and request unnecessary transfers for stage two.

It is possible to combine some of these methods, eg by letting the student start out on a one day a week basis, culminating in a block placement at the end of a term or academic year.

Ultimately, you will decide what is most appropriate for your students. The only caveat we want to issue concerns 'stand alone' block placements of one week.

If you can avoid this, we suggest you do. It is a very short period, only five working days, and this requires just as much time and effort to set up as longer periods of work experience. Employers may dislike it because it disrupts their work pattern, and also because they don't feel it worth giving the student any responsible duties. Students may dislike it for the same reasons, but principally because they have to leave just as they are settling in. Think back to your first week in a new job – things were probably just beginning to swim into focus by Friday.

The only exception to this may be some students with special needs who require a sheltered and shorter placement.

FINDING THE PLACEMENTS

For most organisers of work experience, finding the placements is probably the main issue, and the one which causes most potential headaches. Even if there is a full-time work experience coordinator to help, you will necessarily be involved in some of the location, organisation and administration of placements. If you are operating alone the task may seem overwhelming, especially if you are starting from scratch, with no initial bank of sympathetic employers.

Table 2.2 (page 28) gives many sources of potential placements. You may be able to supplement this from your own local knowledge or even by going on 'walkabout' around town and noting likely addresses. It is amazing how many likely employers can be found by taking the names of companies listed outside large office blocks, for instance.

One dilemma may rear its ugly head: do you use friends as placement employers? In general we would caution against this. However well-meaning your friend and however well motivated your student, if things go wrong you'll kick yourself!

Once you have a list of potential employers, how do you go about getting in touch? There are three main methods. Which you use may vary according to individual circumstances. Many people use a combination of all three techniques.

1 Letter
A standard letter (see Appendices 2.1 and 2.2, pages 33 and 34) sent to as many employers as possible could be the most straightforward method. Sample 2.1 is geared to post-16 students, and sample 2.2 to pre-16 school students. Employers generally appreciate being given some background information about the students, the course they are following, and the school or college they are attending. It is intended that sample (1) be accompanied by some 'course

Table 2.2 *Contacts for work experience*

Directories/handbooks
Yellow Pages; Thomson Local Directories; Kelly's Directory; local community handbooks; recruitment directories; company-sponsored handbooks.

Newspapers/magazines
Local press, including free papers; national press; trade journals, recruitment magazines.

Voluntary organisations
Charities; Citizens' Advice Bureaux; church groups; volunteer bureaux; community organisations.

Business groups/trade associations
Rotary, Inner Wheel, etc; Chambers of Commerce; trade fairs; conventions; exhibitions.

School/college contacts
Governors; firms sending students on day release; other local schools and colleges; former pupils/students now in employment or even possibly running their own businesses; parents (we do not recommend that students do work experience with family members, but parents can be a source of placements for other students.)

Other education contacts
SCIP; LEA work experience coordinators, Project Trident.

Information and resource centres
Careers offices; job centres; teachers' resource centres; libraries.

Training/professional bodies
Industrial training boards; employers' federations; trade associations; professional bodies.

Local councils
Specialist units, eg Economic Development; Planning; Small Businesses.

---

details', as many employers will not be familiar with vocational college courses like 'BTEC National Diploma in Science'. If you decide to go for this 'mailshot' approach, remember the following points:

- Be sure that your letter is concise, to the point and jargon-free. This also holds good for any information/publicity material enclosed with it. If it looks like junk mail, it will go the way of junk mail – unread and in the bin.
- Many employers are not conversant with educational terms and this is not the time to blind them with science. Steer clear of phrases such as 'modular course of study' and 'integration of our cross-curricular approach'.
- Letters may produce only two or three replies out of every ten sent out. This rate is likely to increase if you provide a reply slip and, if possible, a pre-paid return envelope.
- Ensure good quality presentation.
- You may well have to chase up your letter with a phone call (see 2 below). This does mean that when you eventually reach the right person, they may be guiltily aware that they have

not responded to your letter, currently nestling at the bottom of their in-tray. In these circumstances, a positive response may well be forthcoming.

2 Telephone

In theory this is the most immediate way of negotiating a quick response. In practice, it can involve a great deal of being shunted around different departments. These are the points to consider:

- Use a 'script' if you want to ensure that all essential points are covered.
- Beware zealous receptionists/secretaries who are trying to protect their boss from unwanted callers. Establish straightaway that you are not a jobseeker, employment bureau or sales person.
- When 'your' contact is finally located, he/she will probably be in a meeting.
- Don't ring off without ascertaining the name of your contact and when they are likely to be available if you call back.
- It is best to call the employer back rather than request them to contact you. Work experience may be top of your priorities, but it probably comes a long way down the employer's list. If you have promised to phone back, do so, or the employer will think that his/her assistance is no longer required and will give the placement to someone more organised.

    This tenet holds good throughout the negotiations: if an employer promises to get in touch, it is fairly safe to assume that he/she won't (we especially recommend that you do not rely on people to pass on messages).

    Employers may even, at a later stage, forget the commitment they have made or muddle your request with that of another institution.

    Remember that you are like a medieval knight trying to win his lady: you must woo your employer with all the ardour at your command.
- The moral of the above is to confirm any phone conversation in writing as soon as possible, detailing what was discussed, especially date and type of placement.

3 Cold calling/drop-in visits

In other words, calling in to firms without a prior appointment. Remember:

- This approach is only successful for those who feel at home with it.
- It requires good presentation and verbal skills.
- At the very least, it will enable you to leave written details with the employer.
- At best, you will be able to negotiate a placement on the spot.
- The success rate is probably highest with smaller businesses, with firms used to dealing with the public (eg hotels, travel agents) and in industries where informality is the norm.
- It enables a look at the firm without arranging a formal visit.
- Go equipped with back-up material, eg a notebook, letters, leaflets and, if possible, a business card.
- As with the phone-call method, follow up with a letter.

HARD-TO-FIND PLACEMENTS

Certain employers and industries are more amenable to taking students on placement than others. Unfortunately, students often request work experience in job areas where placements are at a premium. Record companies, art studios, etc, are inundated with requests and often cannot help. Added to which, these are often the industries where only the brightest and the best survive, so your shy fifth former may not be the most suitable person to take up any placements which are going.

It is best to temper ambition with realism: if you do manage to obtain such a placement, hang on to it by sending someone with flair and initiative who can cope with – and gain from – high-pressure work.

If you are having difficulty finding a particular type of placement, *think laterally*. The local zoo may be unable to help, but veterinary surgeries, farms (city and rural) and kennels may offer suitable alternatives.

Similarly, if you cannot find anything suitable in journalism, remember that many large companies, including charities and local councils, have their own in-house magazines and PR departments. Bookshops, newsagents and printers could also provide related work experience. Likewise with legal sections, computer facilities, etc.

One problem when making a first approach to an employer is *whom* to contact. Ideally, you will have a name, otherwise address your request to the manager (if it is a small firm) or the personnel manager (larger organisation). With the latter, a written request does run the risk of getting lost in the internal mail system, especially if there is more than one personnel manager or even more than one personnel department.

Many companies are now appointing staff who are responsible for organising work experience, usually in conjunction with other personnel duties. Others will refer you to area office or even to national headquarters.

It is partly because of all these variations on a theme that we suggest that you keep accurate notes of where, when and how contacts are made when canvassing for placements.

RECORD-KEEPING

It is very difficult to organise a successful work experience scheme if you keep notes on the back of an envelope or if miscellaneous pieces of paper are 'filed' all over the building. You will need certain basic documentation:

- A standard canvass letter.
- A publicity brochure (optional).
- A canvass list, recording dates and details of whom you have contacted, what their response has been and any follow-up work done.

You will also need:

- Various follow-up letters (for phone calls, cold canvassing, etc).
- A placement description form.
- A monitoring form.
- An *aide-mémoire* (optional).

- A letter of confirmation.
- A student handout (optional).
- A letter to parents of younger students.
- An employer report form.
- A student feedback form.
- A thank you letter.

Examples of most of these materials are given in the relevant parts of the text.

You will also have to set up a central filing system. Here are four suggested methods of collating the necessary information:

1   Loose-leaf file(s)
Arranged alphabetically and/or by industry. All information relating to employers can be stored in this way although it may eventually run to several hefty tomes.

2   Drop-file
Operated on the same basis as 1. It has the added advantage that bulkier items such as student projects and employer brochures can be stored too.

3   Card index system
With employer details on the front (leave space to update names of contacts, etc), and room for dates, student details and notes on the back. This method can be used in conjunction with 1 and 2 if wished.

4   Computer system
If you are lucky enough to have this resource, make sure that it is user friendly and seek expert help when setting it up. There are now several commercial packages and programs available or you may prefer to dream up your own tailor-made program. In this case, ensure that you have sufficient 'fields' to add, amend and update details. Ideally, there should also be a good 'search' facility on the computer, eg one which can identify placements in certain districts or in specific industries.

If you choose a commercial package, what you buy is going to depend on a variety of factors, not least your budget. Most software packages are pretty reasonably priced and there is a fair amount of choice – which is growing all the time. Suppliers range from established careers publishers such as COIC to those produced by software houses and others which were originally formulated on a local basis. Veryan, for instance, is a commercially produced, dedicated software package designed specifically for the running of work experience programmes. It enables virtually all aspects of work experience organisation to be handled by computer, from printing address labels for your mailshot through to matching student requirements with available placements. Training and back-up support is also offered in the deal. It is the type of system which can be used by individual schools and colleges as well as by work experience coordinators offering a centralised service to a number of institutions. On the other hand WEXIS, which is the product of an educational background, performs a similar range of functions and has also been regarded as highly successful. It was developed by North Tyneside Careers Service in conjunction with TVEI and the DTI. We mention those two systems only as examples of the wide range available. Do shop around before deciding and choose something which suits both your circumstances and your pocket.

However you decide to keep your records, try to see that they are accessible to anyone else who needs to use them. Also remember that there may be occasions when students, parents and employers want access to these files.

APPENDIX 2.1 Initial canvass letter to employers (1) (Post-16 students) – for approaching new employers

Date as postmark

Dear Sir/Madam,

At this college we are planning to run a work experience programme for the BTEC National Diploma in Science course.

Students, who are mainly in the 16–19 age group, will spend three weeks in unpaid placements with local employers from 1–19 March.

I enclose course details, from which you can see that students are covering practical and academic skills, equivalent to A level. They will be seeking work or entering higher education when they complete the course next year.

If your organisation could help by providing a placement(s), please contact me by letter or telephone or by completing the attached reply slip.

I will then be pleased to discuss matters further and provide fuller details.

Thank you for your interest. I look forward to hearing from you,

Yours faithfully,

APPENDIX 2.2 Initial canvass letter to employers (2) (Pre-16 students) – for approaching new employers

Date

Dear

re – Work Experience Placements for Students

As Work Experience Coordinator for Southside School I am writing to ask if you are willing to consider accepting one of our pupils into your workplace for short periods of unpaid work experience?

Work Experience is an important part of pupils' preparation for life and work, designed to help them mature and be better prepared for the world of work. We would be very grateful indeed for your support in offering placements. We basically ask that you offer young people the opportunity to experience a real working environment and a normal working day, while giving them the supervision and support appropriate for a young person having their first taste of working life.

Would you be kind enough to complete and return the enclosed form?

On receiving your replies I will contact you again to give you further information about, and discuss with you, the particular pupil I would like to place with you. In most instances a pupil's CV will be sent, and I will arrange for the pupil to meet you before the placement begins. We might also have a chat over the phone.

It would also help to have some general information about your organisation and the kind of activities a pupil might do on work experience. This information will help me to identify a suitable pupil, and help the pupil have a realistic expectation of the placement.

I do hope these arrangements are satisfactory and that you feel able to support our work experience programme. Please do not hesitate to contact me if you have any queries or comments or would like to suggest other ways in which we can help you to help us/our pupils.

May I assure you of the high value we place on the contribution you can make to the education of our young people and of our appreciation of the time and effort you give to our pupils.

Yours faithfully,

3

Preparation

Most organisers of work experience heave a sigh of relief when the first offers of placements start to materialise. This is, after all, an achievement in itself. However, it is not by any means the end of the matter. Tempting though it may be to sit back and relax, you are now ready to move on to the next phase of the operation: preparation.

This means preparation of *all* parties involved in the work experience – not only the students but the employers, your fellow teachers and the students' parents or guardians (see eg Appendices 3.17–3.20 on pages 79–83). Again, this might seem like a lot of extra work, but it will pay dividends once the placements are underway.

Chronologically, the first group of people to be involved in the preparation process are the employers.

THE EMPLOYER

Pre-visits to employers

If you are operating in ideal circumstances (and this may be the exception rather than the rule) either you or another member of staff or the LEA work experience coordinator will immediately respond to an offer of a new placement by arranging a visit to the employer's premises, armed with a brief introduction for employers like the one reproduced at the end of this Chapter (see Appendix 3.1, page 54). A copy of this can be given to students when allocating placements. You could also usefully take with you a leaflet on the lines of employers' notes for guidance, as shown in Appendix 3.2, page 56.

The main purposes of this visit are:

1   To meet the employer and establish friendly relations
There are several benefits to this course of action:

– It is usually much appreciated by employers who do not always understand the constraints of the timetable and may equate failure to visit with lack of interest.

2   To nurture the employer and negotiate placement details

It is much easier and quicker to exchange information, explain objectives and finalise plans on a face-to-face basis than it is by any other method. This often enables a more varied placement timetable to be drawn up, by establishing that the work experience could go to a student who has specific skills or aptitudes – such as typing, computing or the ability to work with the public.

- You can iron out any potential misunderstandings about the tasks to be allocated. For instance, you may feel that the duties mentioned by the employer are too easy or, alternatively, too onerous for one of your students. Or the employer may point out that certain types of job cannot be done by those on work experience. It would, for example, be reasonable to suppose that students placed in a bank or building society would be handling cash, but this is often not the case.
- You may discover that there are as yet unexplored possibilities of additional placements in other departments. Explore them. It may present an opportunity to secure the placement for other students in the future.
- This is a less formal way to raise any potentially difficult issues, whether they are to do with individual students or centre around areas like interviews or the possibility of the employer contributing towards lunches, fares, etc. Can the employer provide safety boots, uniform skirts, etc, or will the student have to buy these?

3   To brief the employer about the students, course and school

Information about the particular student you wish to place can be given later, but this is a useful opportunity to provide the employer with a broad idea of the general academic level, expectations and maturity of students, the nature of the course they are following, the skills they have, etc.

4   To clinch and confirm the placement

Human nature being what it is, an employer is far less likely to forget about your placement or let you down at the eleventh hour if he/she has met you in person and you are no longer just a disembodied voice at the end of a phone or a scrawled signature on a standard letter.

5   To check the suitability of the placement for your purposes and your students

Contrary to popular imagination, work experience is not generally offered by firms looking for cheap labour whose staff and premises exist in conditions of Dickensian squalor. However, one or two 'cowboys' do occasionally rear their ugly heads and a visit should allow you to discover this before matters have a chance to proceed any further.

6   To vet the placement and the workplace

A visit allows you to ensure that placements found by students themselves *do* fit the bill and that these employers know the purpose of the placement and what it will entail for them.

- You can check out the health and safety situation. Appendix 3.3 on page 58 is a useful *aide-mémoire*. It is intended as an awareness raiser for teachers – a checklist of things to be alert to when visiting employers' premises – certainly not as a list of questions to ask employers. You generally need only politely ask employers to draw to the attention of work experience placees any health and safety matters which they should be aware of. You may also want to note if the premises and facilities are suitable for disabled students.
- You may wish to check certain arrangements which could affect the student's welfare, eg if

shifts are being worked (not unusual in leisure centres, hotels, etc), how easy or safe will travelling be?

- A visit will also allow you to assess the firm in other less tangible ways too, and is a means of discovering things that might otherwise remain unknown, such as the atmosphere in the workplace – relaxed or informal, pressurised or slower paced? Does it seem to be a supportive environment for your less confident students or would it suit someone more outgoing?

- Is the workforce fairly well balanced in terms of gender and ethnic origin? If not, does this have any implications? A lack of, say, female or Afro-Caribbean staff may not necessarily be significant, but should be noted. At best, it should be pointed out to students who might otherwise feel ill at ease in, eg, an all-white or all-female atmosphere; at worst, it may be the outward manifestation of racism or sexism.

- While on this tack, it is more likely that racist or sexist attitudes will come to light during a visit than when a placement is arranged 'at a distance'. Without a visit, the problem may only arise when the student attends for a pre-placement visit or interview or, even worse, when he/she is actually *in situ*. These issues will be covered in more detail in Chapter 6, but it is as well to be aware of them at this stage.

Written communication with employers

You will also want to confirm details in writing once the placement has been allocated. This could well be a long time after your visit and may also follow a pre-placement interview, but as it still falls under the heading of employer preparation, examples of confirmatory letters and a confirmation reply slip can be found in Appendices 3.5, 3.6 and 3.7 on pages 61–4. Clearly it would be possible to add embellishments if you wished, eg the name of the monitoring tutor, the hours of work, but our examples cover all salient points and you have to insert nothing more complicated and time-consuming than the relevant dates and the names of both parties involved.

Insurance and indemnity

The confirmatory letter should be accompanied by a brief guide for employers on the lines set out in Figure 3.1, plus *an indemnity form and an insurance form* (see Figures 3.2 and 3.3). These are a vital part of the mechanics of work experience. The indemnity covers employers against loss, injury or damage (whether malicious or unintentional) while the student is with them and agrees to meet any claim *for which the LEA is found to be liable*. It is a legal document, drawn up by lawyers and the wording may vary slightly from LEA to LEA. The example in Figure 3.2 comes from the now defunct ILEA. As with the parental consent forms which are mentioned later in this chapter, *you should not alter or expand the wording in any way as this may render it invalid*. Some LEAs have indemnity forms which cover educational visits. *Do not use these for work experience.*

At present, indemnity is generally offered by LEAs, which also generally have personal accident insurance covering all pupils and students on work experience. With local management of schools, responsibility for insurance and indemnity *may* pass from the LEA to the school. Similarly, when colleges of further education go out of LEA control, the responsibility

THE WORK EXPERIENCE MANUAL

for insurance and indemnity may also pass to the individual institution. *You are therefore strongly advised to check what arrangements are in place in your area and in your institution.*

The whole issue of indemnity and insurance should be discussed with the employer (see

Figure 3.1 *A brief guide for employers: insurance, indemnity and health and safety on work experience*

OLDSHIRE EDUCATION AUTHORITY
WORK EXPERIENCE
Insurance, indemnity and health and safety on work experience – a brief guide for employers

Pupils and students on work experience are covered under the Health and Safety at Work Act.

The Education Authority provides Personal Accident Insurance which automatically covers all pupils/students on work experience.

The Education Authority also indemnifies employers against any injury, loss or damage incurred as a result of the placement (unless the employer is negligent).

Virtually all employers are required by law to have Employer's Liability Insurance. This also normally covers pupils/students on work experience. *You should inform your insurance company that you intend to take pupils/students on work experience.*

Figure 3.2 *Specimen indemnity form*

To:
The Inner London Education Authority (hereafter called 'The Authority') hereby requests you to permit

....

students from

....

to assist in the carrying on of your business for the purposes of practical training on

....

and in consideration of your so doing the Authority hereby agrees to indemnify you and your servants and agents from and against all liability for personal injury (whether fatal or otherwise), loss of or damage to property and any other loss or damage (other than injury, loss or damage caused or contributed by the negligence of yourself, your servants or agents) resulting from the said permission, provided that nothing in the foregoing shall exclude or restrict the operation of Section 47(2) of the Health and Safety at Work Act 1974, or any liability arising thereunder except as may be otherwise provided in health and safety regulations as defined in the Act.

Dated this .... day of ....

(Signed) ....

Table 3.1). Experienced placement providers will probably raise the matter themselves. There is no need to be alarmist about this – the majority of placements pass off peacefully and the indemnity is only rarely used for anything other than minor damages to people or property. Nevertheless, as the cautionary tale below illustrates, major problems *can* happen and the indemnity does not cover every circumstance. For this reason, you should suggest that employers check whether their own insurance provision (employer's liability and, in many cases, public/third party liability) covers students on work experience. In most cases, any insurance which does not meet these needs can be extended. Most employers' liability

Figure 3.3 *Employer's liability insurance*

Employer's liability – confirmation of cover
As an Authority we have a duty to ensure that the employers we use for work experience do have Employer's Liability Insurance, where required.

Would you be good enough to complete and return this slip to: ....

I can confirm that this organisation has Employer's Liability and that it is extended to cover pupils/students on work experience.
YES/NO*   *delete as approp.

This organisation is exempt from the requirement to have Employer's Liability Insurance on the following grounds (please tick as approp.):

– Crown undertaking
– do not employ anyone
– domestic household
– National Health Service

Name of organisation ....

Address ....

Signed .... Date ....

Position in organisation ....

With thanks.

Table 3.1 *Insurance cover: questions for employers*

---

1 Does their insurance policy cover students on work experience?
2 Which insurance company do they use?
3 Will the students travel in any company vehicles?
4 Will they be insured while doing so?
5 Details of vehicles, eg do they have fixed seats?
6 Will the students be insured for work done off the firm's premises?

---

insurance does cover students on work experience, but employers should be advised to check this and to inform their insurers that they are taking on work experience students. However, some organisations such as the NHS and Crown undertakings are not required to have employer's liability, although other arrangements may be in place.

Indemnity: a cautionary tale

A student on a vocational course was on placement with a firm whose brief occasionally involved doing repair work in private homes. The student sometimes accompanied skilled staff on these jobs and, after one such visit, the householder found that some expensive jewellery was missing. Police traced some of the items to the student's possession, but not everything was recovered. The householder claimed compensation from the firm, which then contacted the college, which had, in good faith, sent the student to them. The LEA lawyers would not make any payment to the firm because the incident had not happened 'on employer's premises' as specified on the indemnity form. The householder, perhaps understandably, decided to prosecute the student who, in consequence, ended up with a criminal record. And no one lived happily ever after.

We hope that you have now been persuaded (or have persuaded others) of the necessity of making an initial visit. Certainly for students of compulsory school age, all placements should be checked by a pre-placement visit. But if your time is at a premium, you will have to try and establish most of the salient facts by phone or letter. It is still a good idea to complete a placement description form (see Appendix 3.4, page 59), which can be filed in your own record-keeping system and a copy given to the student when the placement is allocated.

Some canny operators send the form to the employer to complete and, while this is a good time-management ploy, it does mean that details obtained in this fashion are likely to be selective. The completed form can also be passed on to the teacher who is monitoring the work experience. Not only should it provide a background to the monitoring visit, but the teacher should also be able to supplement the information and fill in any gaps (see footnote to Appendix 3.4)

Which brings is to the next group of people who will need to be prepared for what is ahead – colleagues.

COLLEAGUES

If you have followed the suggestions in Chapter 2, your fellow workers should be fairly clued up as to why work experience is taking place, how it is organised and what their role is likely to be.

Staff training

We have constantly mentioned the need for staff to be kept informed of developments on the work experience programme and to be given guidelines on how to deal with the various situations that can arise before, during and after placements. We appreciate that most of this work may be carried out in an informal setting, but there may be instances when you need to offer formal training, such as INSET, to your colleagues on some of the key issues.

The chapter on Monitoring, together with its accompanying materials, in themselves provide a good basis for any such training, but here we make a few suggestions about what could be covered in a comprehensive programme or in individual sessions. If you are lucky enough to be given a number of sessions to run, these are the issues you should aim to cover:

- Equal opportunities.
- Health and safety, and insurance.
- Monitoring and record-keeping.
- Organising work experience.
- Designing work-based assignments.

Clearly, you may not want to do all this single-handed. Outside help can be coopted, eg speakers from the Education Department on insurance, from a local branch of the Health and Safety Executive, or the LEA equal opportunities coordinators.

Figure 3.4 *Health and safety questionnaire*

---

1 Have you had any training in health and safety?
Yes [ ]   No [ ]
2 Give two examples of situations covered by the Health and Safety at Work Act.

3 Does the Act apply to your students on work experience?
Yes [ ]   No [ ]   Don't know [ ]
4 Could the work done by your students on placement be potentially hazardous?
Yes [ ]   No [ ]
5 Do your students have to wear protective clothing on work experience?
Yes [ ]   No [ ]   If Yes, what and why?

6 Have any of your students had and accident on placement?
Yes [ ]   No [ ]   If Yes, what caused it?

7 Do most of the firms your students go to on placement have:
(a) an accident book?   Yes [ ]   No [ ]
(b) a safety rep/committee? Yes [ ]   No [ ]
8 Do you feel certain that your students are adequately protected against health and safety hazards while on work experience?
Yes [ ]   No [ ]
9 What advice on health and safety would you give to students before they go on work experience?

Equal Opportunities is probably best approached via role plays. You could use the case studies in Appendix I, page 130, or role plays featured in the text (see Appendix 3.15, page 75) or ask the group to imagine one or all of the following situations:

- A student returning to school/college before the end of the placement and refusing to talk about his/her experiences.
- A phone conversation with an employer clearly reluctant to take on a student apparently for reasons of gender/race.
- A visit to an employer who may have been discriminating against a student on placement.

Health and safety and insurance issues can again centre around material elsewhere in the book such as Table 3.1 (page 39) and the health and safety checklist (Appendix 3.3, page 58), but Figure 3.4 (page 41) may be useful to get colleagues thinking.

Monitoring and record-keeping. The placement description form (Appendix 3.4, page 59) and monitoring *aide-mémoire* for staff (Appendix 4.2, page 94) are the obvious foundations for this session, which could be supplemented by considering various role plays/case studies. The record-keeping element can be approached either by going through the various documents and/or computer records or by asking staff to design their own materials/programmes.

Organising work experience. This can centre around the time chart in Chapter 2 (Table 2.1, page 22) or around the contacts for work experience (Table 2.2, page 28). To focus the group on to this activity Exercise 3.1 (below) can be done alone or in pairs, followed by a feedback session. Aims to be stressed include:

- The need for students to experience both working life and the socialisation process.
- To expand career horizons.

Exercise 3.1 *Organising work experience*

A. Outline a specific student group:

- Age
- Course
- Level
- Length of placement
- Reason for placement

B. Identify three or four main aims for your work experience programme:

1.

2.

3.

4.

- To increase students' confidence.
- To allow the student, where appropriate, to learn specific skills, obtain references, make contacts.

Designing work-based assignments. Based on the stated aims and objectives from Exercise 3.1, the group should be asked to design materials around student preparation or work experience diaries, both discussed in Chapter 3.

If you are designing a leaflet or information pack for students going on work experience, it will obviously vary according to your 'audience'. In the sample in Appendix 3.8 on page 65, we cover the questions that students most commonly ask and suggest some answers which can be adapted to your own circumstances. The leaflet could stand alone, or also be used in preparatory sessions.

PARENTS

Preparation of parents is also key to the success of work experience. As we have said in an earlier chapter, parents may perceive work experience as a kind of pre-employment trial period and feel affronted or angry if the placement does not match the careers aspirations they have for their offspring. Their understanding of the educational aims of work experience and their commitment to them, need to be ensured. They have an important role to play in encouraging their daughters and sons to value the opportunity being offered them and to approach it with enthusiasm. On a more practical level, they need to be made aware of the importance of appropriate dress on work experience, time-keeping, punctuality, reporting in when sick and so on – just as if their sons and daughters were starting a new job. Some parents mistakenly believe this is not so important when their children are not being paid. One needs to recognise, however, that students' domestic circumstances are not always supportive of students' or indeed parents' best intentions. Single-parent families, parents who work shifts, or leave the home for work before their children do, lack of access to a telephone, either at home or at work, and a myriad of other problems can put work experience lower down the agenda than one would ideally like it to be. Nevertheless, parents' support should be sought and nurtured as far as possible.

The materials in Appendices 3.17 to 3.20 (parents' letter and parents' contract) are intended to reinforce and formalise an understanding which has already been reached between school and parents. A special parents' evening may be arranged specifically to talk about work experience and answer parents' questions. Alternatively, or additionally, the teacher responsible for work experience may wish to take an opportunity during a more general parents' evening to make a presentation on work experience, or to make themselves available to meet parents individually to discuss their child's placement or deal with their concerns. (This does not, of course, address the problem of those parents who do not attend parents' evenings. The parents' letter and parents' contract can in themselves help raise awareness and understanding.) Other teaching staff can also be encouraged to bring work experience into their discussions with parents whenever the opportunity presents itself. This of course hinges on *their* awareness of work experience and on work experience having a high profile in the school generally.

And so on to the final group of people who need preparation – the students.

STUDENTS

As with parents and guardians, the idea of work experience should not just be thrust upon them. It should be accepted as an integral part of both their course of study and their careers education. Work experience should be frequently mentioned, well in advance, in course literature, careers talks, and lessons. When the time for work experience approaches, students should be informed of the projected dates as early as possible.

Your approach to student preparation is going to vary according to the age, ability and numbers of the classes involved. However, a word of caution. Never assume that older or more academic students will necessarily be more geared up about work experience. Some women returners, for instance, may well lack confidence in their ability to cope with working life or they may be worried that working hours will disrupt their domestic arrangements. A-level students can be just as ignorant about the world of work and just as unrealistic in their aspirations as can fourth formers, while some 14-year-olds have a very mature approach.

One way of helping any group of students get matters into perspective is to ask them to make a formal application to you for work experience (see Appendices 3.9, 3.10 and 3.11 on pages 66–9). This will:

– Obtain necessary written details with minimum inconvenience to yourself.
– Form the basis of subsequent individual discussions with students.
– Provide a foundation for the finding and allocation of placements.
– Form the basis for group-work sessions/role play.
– Get the students thinking seriously about work experience and its implications.

Even talking the students through these forms is a useful exercise. *They* may not have been aware, for example, that health considerations, such as colour blindness or short sight, could restrict their choice of placement. *You* need to know practical details, such as those specified, before you can finalise placements. *Employers* should be told if it is likely that the student cannot work normal placement hours. Some employers will be open to negotiation on this, others will not. Either way, it is best that the matter is raised at an early stage, rather than the week before work experience starts – or a few hours into the placement.

Two other major points can be noted from the forms:

1   The attitude of individual students towards work experience: some may be blasé or non-committal about it, but other reactions, such as hostility or extreme nervousness, need to be discussed straightaway.

2   The choice of work experience: the aims and objectives behind work experience do need to be explained before the forms are completed, so that the students understand that job sampling is not the main issue. You may also have to inject an air of realism into the proceedings. Even as this is being written, recollections flood back of the boy who wanted to be a pilot for three

weeks! This does *not* mean that you should veto anything out of the ordinary, but that students should be asked to assess what they can sensibly expect to achieve in the given time as well as weighing up what is feasible locally. Some basic careers research can – and should – form part of the run up to work experience. By all means let someone put forward the idea of graphic artist, if there is nothing to indicate that this is out of the question, but try to ensure that at least one of the other choices relates to a more readily available job area. If the three areas listed read something like disc jockey, photographer and cartoonist, you know that you're in trouble!

This brings us on to a related issue:

Students finding their own placements

There are three possible settings for handing this task over to the 'consumers':

1   Some schools and colleges insist that all students find – or at least attempt to find – their own work experience as an integral part of the whole exercise. In practice, this usually means that they locate employers who might be willing to take them on placement and it is up to you to do any necessary follow up.
2   Alternatively, some students may volunteer to find their own placements because they already have ideas about/contacts in areas where they would like to work.
3   Finally, you may feel that this approach would be appropriate for an individual student or students, perhaps because they are ready to do so or because it will help them to develop certain skills. Or it could just be that they have asked for work experience in a very difficult or narrow area and you feel that you will not have the resources to pursue such an esoteric choice. In this case, it is well to point out to the student that most placements which fall into this category (eg journalism, advertising, film studios) would actively *prefer* the first contact to come from the student. This is because it shows a certain amount of tenacity and enterprise on their part and these are qualities which are necessary to 'make it' in those careers.

Whatever the reason, the students will need a lot of support. In fact, it may not mean less work for you. You may like to help them:

– By ensuring that they are well prepared and that they understand the aims and objectives behind the work experience. If students are vague about this, the employers are going to be even less well informed.
– By giving them the contacts for work experience listed in Chapter 2 (Table 2.2, page 28) and also by spending at least one session with them on the ways of researching and approaching possible contacts (again see Chapter 2).
– By laying down a strict timetable for them to follow – and making them stick to it. Very few students are going to be inclined to approach employers straightaway and it is the sort of thing that gets shelved as non-urgent when class work and social life take priority. Set deadlines and/or put aside lesson time for them to approach *and* follow up contacts. If they have not progressed very far by this pre-arranged date, you will have to step in to ascertain what is happening and, frequently, to rescue the placement or find a new one. You certainly will not be able to rely on all of your charges being successful.

- By giving them what employers will see as 'official backing'. If students are contacting organisations by phone, this may amount to no more than authorising (indeed encouraging them) to use your name and that of the school/college during the conversation. For personal/ mailshot approaches, this can be translated into a written statement in a letter drawn up by the student (see Figure 3.5 for a model). The alternative is a standard letter signed by yourself – but why create more paperwork? As long as the student's letter is neat and on headed notepaper, the overall effect looks official and professional as well as being personal to that student.

Figure 3.5 *Student's canvass letter to employer*

Address
Date

Dear Sir/Madam,

I am a student at St Oswald's College and I am in the first year of my BTEC National course in Business and Computer Studies.
As part of the course, I must do two weeks' unpaid work experience which will count towards my final grade. As I have always been interested in legal work, I wonder whether it would be possible to spend my fortnight's placement (from Monday, 13 May to Friday, 24 May) with your organisation?
Please find enclosed my CV which provides further details about my education and interests.
I hope that you will be able to offer me a placement. If you need more information about the work experience and what it involves, my course tutor Ms Carole Edwards will be pleased to help. She can be contacted at the above address or by phone on 123 4567.
Thank you for your interest. I look forward to hearing from you.

Yours faithfully,

It is a good idea to enclose a CV. Not only will it certainly impress an employer, it is a useful careers exercise and will set the students thinking about their own skills and achievements. Properly presented, it will provide the sort of information which may help the student to obtain the placement. In 'Lee Kempson's' case (Appendix 3.10, page 68), it shows acceptable educational achievements, a wide range of interests, a responsible part-time job and evidence of interest in the law.

As has been amply demonstrated, the fact that some or all of your students are identifying their own placements may not save you much effort, although it will certainly redistribute the workload and should enable students to feel more involved in the whole process.

Three points should be stressed here:

1   Unless there are special circumstances, it is not a good idea for students to use their part-

time jobs or family firms for work experience. Part of the rationale behind the idea of going out on placement is to come into contact with *new* people, places and experiences.

2 If a student has identified a placement at a firm hitherto unknown to you, then it is a priority that, whenever possible, you visit that firm to ascertain that it is suitable. Hopefully, it will be and you can add it to 'your' bank of placements, but if not, it would be best to discover this at an early stage.

3 Every placement, whether student-generated or not, will require the same amount of paperwork and documentation.

Hard-to-place students

There will always be a few students whom, for one reason or another, you are wary about sending out on work experience, or who prove difficult to place. Some work experience coordinators keep a cache of supportive employers to deal with this very contingency. We look at specific cases which may present difficulties in Chapter 6 on Special Issues. But for many of you, the main problem is students who lack motivation on work experience. You feel that they are likely to prove lazy, disruptive, poor timekeepers (possibly all three) while away from your eagle eye. Do you take the risk and send them out or do you look for alternatives?

It is not always possible to predict who is going to cause problems on work experience. Trouble, of whatever sort, can come from the most unlikely quarters, while students who seemed recipes for disaster turn out fine. In a new environment, away from peer group pressure and entrusted with responsibility, they rise to the occasion. Any potential cause(s) for concern should be raised with the student and, if necessary, bargains can be struck along the lines of 'hand in your assignments on time/turn up for class and you can go to X on work experience.'

Some students do respond to this method even though it may smack of bribery and corruption! But if you decide to give the student the benefit of the doubt, do you forewarn the employer? Yes, but don't lay it on too thick. 'Lee Kempson has a problem with timekeeping, but will be turning over a new leaf for work experience' is the recommended approach, rather than 'Lee Kempson is never on time and had better be sent straight back to us if there are any problems'.

If you are genuinely unable to send a student out or a placement breaks down at the last moment, what do you do? We suggest a contingency plan based on a reciprocal arrangement with neighbouring schools, colleges or other education organisations such as teachers' centres. Staff here are more likely to be sympathetic to the situation, but they too have jobs to get on with, so make sure that you or your opposite number there keeps them well primed. Dumping a student in the lab, the office or the reprographics unit with no prior warning does not bode well for any of those concerned.

ALLOCATION OF PLACEMENTS

The next step of the proceedings for students *not* finding their own work experience is allocation of placements. This raises a thorny question: who decides where the students go?

There are two main choices:

1   Some work experience facilitators are happy to let the students themselves decide or even to let a joint decision be taken by a group or class. This can often work well if only small numbers are involved and there is ample time for discussion of individual strengths and weaknesses to be considered. In fact, in these circumstances, it is a good decision-making and self-awareness exercise which covers a lot of the wider aims of work experience. Students can also be asked to do a self-assessment exercise individually. In either event, the classroom session can be based around the questionnaire shown in Appendix 3.12 on page 70 (which can then be used as the basis for a CV).

This method of placement allocation can also turn into a mock job-hunting exercise with students selecting their choices from cards similar to those found in careers offices and job centres. In this case, the placement description form (Appendix 3.4) can serve as a job description.

Inevitably, a dilemma arises if two students opt for the same placement. The casting vote could belong to you, another member of staff or the group. But whichever of these alternatives is used, the final decision should be an informed one, ie the students concerned should have to 'apply', either verbally or in writing, and give reasons for their preference.

2   *You* can throw democracy to the winds and make the final allocation yourself, based on the details on the application for work experience form and your own or other staff's knowledge of the student. In these circumstances, be prepared to give reasons for your choice. If at all possible, students should be given a regular update on the placement finding process, so that if much-sought-after placements don't materialise, feathers won't be too ruffled.

Interviews and visits

Once placements have been allocated, arrangements for interviews and visits can be made. Many employers are very pro interview and will often propose the idea themselves. Most others will be extremely amenable if you suggest such a course. It must be stressed to employers that it is *not* usually a chance for them to select one candidate from a number of students. In most cases you will have done that for them. The only exceptions might be as follows:

- If it is a particularly plum placement and there are several good students interested in it and/ or the nature of the business is such that the employer must be satisfied that the student has certain specific skills before the work experience goes ahead.
- If the placement is to be very lengthy, eg several months, and/or the student will be involved in a particular project.
- If it is intended that the placement will eventually lead to employment, as in the case of YT and ET students.

But generally speaking, the interview will be an opportunity for both student and employer to get to know each other and sort out between themselves the finer points of what the work experience should involve. The interview *aide-mémoire* in Appendix 3.13 (page 71) may be useful here. The meeting is also a chance for the student to practise interview techniques in a 'safe' situation. Often employers will ask them to complete application forms and go through the whole interview procedure precisely so that the students can be given feedback on their performance. This can be a bit daunting, so students should be given a clear idea of whether to expect this or something less formal *before* they set off to see the employer. Whatever the situation, students should be encouraged to prepare their CVs and Records of Achievement and take them along to interview.

Of course, none of this precludes one or both of the parties involved deciding not to proceed with the placement. This may happen only rarely but the student will need careful counselling as to why he/she did not like the placement or why the employer felt them to be unsuitable. The same tenet applies to the employers concerned: if the student, for some perfectly valid reason, does not wish to go on the placement, give the workplace some feedback. Having wooed the employers so ardently, don't just drop them with no explanation.

For some employers and students an interview will not be appropriate, but in this instance, the students should definitely visit the firm to introduce themselves and familiarise themselves with the organisation and its staff. Like the interview, a visit should enable students to use and develop social skills. It is also a practical exercise: the students have to research how to reach the placement and ensure that they arrive on time. Introductions to the people (and equipment) with which they will be working means that they will feel more confident on the first day of the placement, which can otherwise seem very bewildering.

Whether they opt for interviews or visits, it is the students, not you, who should make the

Figure 3.6 *Student's telephone script*

STUDENT: May I speak to Joe Michaels please?
RECEPTIONIST: Who's calling, please?
STUDENT: Lee Kempson.
RECEPTIONIST: What is it about?
STUDENT: I've been asked to call to arrange an interview with him.
RECEPTIONIST: He is in a meeting at the moment. I'll leave a message to say that you called.
STUDENT: Is there a good time to call him back?
RECEPTIONIST: He's free tomorrow afternoon.
STUDENT: Thank you, I'll call back then.

STUDENT: Hello, is that Joe Michaels?
JM: Yes, how can I help you?
STUDENT: My name's Lee Kempson from St Oswald's College, Mr Michaels. My tutor, Carole Edwards, asked me to get in touch to arrange a work experience interview.
JM: Oh yes, you called yesterday, didn't you? Well, can you come round on Monday at 10 o'clock?
STUDENT: I'm sorry, that's not convenient. Could we make it Tuesday at the same time?
JM: Yes that would be fine. Do you know how to get here?
STUDENT: I know the bus stop. Thank you, Mr Michaels. I look forward to seeing you on Tuesday at 10. Goodbye.

---

arrangements by phoning the employer. This may mean training in telephone techniques, and the class or individual students could draw up a 'script' to help them (see Figure 3.6). There are several learning points here: dealing confidently with the receptionist, being clear and concise, being assertive, etc.

Again it is important that students work to a deadline. Often they will defer phoning the employer because they are nervous or they don't feel that it is urgent. They may fondly imagine that the employer is sitting there waiting for them to call and so leave things to the last minute. This does mean a certain amount of chasing up recalcitrant individuals, and some teachers keep a chart – possibly on the classroom wall – listing interview and visit arrangements as they are made.

When students are due to see the employer, they can be given an introduction card or letter (see Figure 3.7) as they would if they were being sent for a real interview by the careers or job centre. This looks professional, fixes the arrangements in the student's mind and can circumvent problems with security staff at the work place.

Figure 3.7 *Student's letter of introduction*

WORK EXPERIENCE PLACEMENT
Newtown High School,
Newtown,
Berks.

To: ....

This is to introduce .... who has an appointment with

you on .... at .... to discuss his/her work experience
placement.

The details are as follows:

Dates of placement: ....

Name of teacher in charge ....

I do hope that you feel able to accommodate the above named pupil for work experience. Please do not hesitate to contact me if there is anything you wish to discuss.
With very many thanks for your support,

Yours sincerely,

THE DIARY

Every student going on work experience should keep some record, usually in the form of a diary or logbook. The exact layout and format will vary according to the type of students involved and your own resources. Below we list some elements that should be contained in most diaries and may also form the basis for specific projects/assignments done on placement. The diary can be started before the placement begins, as details of interviews/visits and background material can be incorporated at this stage.

- Details of placement, contact name, interview arrangements, etc.
- Analysis of interview/visit.
- Record of feelings prior to placement and after day one.
- History/background to organisation and industry.
- Structure/hierarchy of firm and department, eg using charts and/or diagrams. Numbers working in the student's section, roles and responsibilities.
- Career prospects within firm/industry, eg points of entry, qualifications needed, training, etc.
- Environment, eg state of building, physical conditions.
- Conditions and facilities, eg staff canteen, staff benefits, working hours.
- Day-to-day record of tasks done and observed, including new skills learnt and equipment used. Which jobs the student found interesting/routine, easy/difficult, etc.
- Specific projects.
- Job study/studies.
- Trade union arrangements.
- Health and Safety measures, including hygiene rules, equipment used, labelling, storage and movement of materials and equipment, layout and organisation of workspaces, hazards, safety procedures.

If you are dealing with a discrete group of students, eg CPVE Care courses or A-level languages, it may be possible to make the diary more uniform and incorporate certain standard tasks or coursework assignments.

Students will need guidance on completion of the diary before they go out and it should certainly be given to them well in advance of the placement's start date.

A preparation session should be used to go through the diary and its contents and the following points should be emphasised:

- The diary should be completed regularly and be ready to be shown to the monitoring tutor. (NB, very occasionally employers may ask to see the diary, so it may be politic for students to record possibly contentious material elsewhere.)
- Some questions will need to be carefully handled. Most people are very happy to talk about their jobs, but questions centring round pay do need a certain amount of tact. Discuss with the class the most appropriate way of dealing with this. Likewise, if there are poor relations between unions and management, students should tread carefully and be sure to get a balanced view.
- Diaries should be kept up to date and can, with the employer's permission, be completed in work time, eg at slack periods. Otherwise, they should be finished in the student's own time. We remember the student who, in all earnestness, told her supervisor that she would not have time to do a particular task as she had to write up her diary!

CLASSROOM PREPARATION SESSIONS

The preceding sections of this chapter have provided plenty of material for working with groups of students. Activities such as finding placements or preparing for interviews can be tailored to the time and resources available to you. Often they can be supplemented by discussions and also by traditional careers materials on presentation skills, first days at work, careers videos, etc. Even though work experience is currently such a growth area, there is very little in the way of audio-visual materials specifically aimed at this market. (Enterprising media resources departments, please note.)

However, there will be many other items which you want to bring to your students' attention before they embark on their placements. These can be built into an actual preparation programme to run parallel with the activities listed earlier, or they may have to be condensed into a few sessions. Whichever options are open to you, below is a list of topics which should be covered before the work experience takes place. Suggestions for how to tackle each subject are also given, as are some possible scenarios for role play exercises. To illustrate the sort of written preparation which could be done, we have given an example about timekeeping (often cited by employers as a cause for concern) in Appendix 3.14 on page 73.

1   The mechanics of work experience: monitoring arrangements – and all students should know the name of their monitoring tutor, and why they will be visited, before the placement starts; what to do if they are sick – generally this means contacting both workplace and school/ college; what to do if unexpected problems arise, etc.
2   Duties on work experience: remind students that every job carries its share of routine duties and that work experience students will have to do their quota. This does not mean that they should be condemned to do the filing or make the tea for days on end, but they cannot expect instant responsibility. Some firms deliberately start all students off on fairly basic work and 'promote' them only when they have performed these duties well. (See Appendix 3.15, Role Play One, page 75.)
3   Social skills: this can cover something as simple as the importance of good timekeeping, often a major issue on work experience, to negotiating skills when, for instance, the student wants to change some aspect of the work experience. The importance of good communication skills and the need to be assertive rather than aggressive or shy can be incorporated into this. The need to *ask questions* should also be stressed. Often otherwise normally outgoing students are diffident about this. They don't want to seem stupid or pester people needlessly, but can cause havoc if they attempt tasks which they do not understand properly. This attitude can affect non-work areas too: we know of one bright 18-year-old who didn't go to lunch for the first three days of her placement because no one had told her where the canteen was.

Using anecdotes such as this and role play exercises can help illustrate common dilemmas which most students won't even have considered (see Appendix 3.15, Role Plays Three to Five pages 76–7). Discussion could also centre around what students perceive to be the main difficulties which may arise on placement. Many students are nervous about going to an unfamiliar environment and their concerns are often connected with communications and social skills.

Splitting students into groups and asking them to feed back on particular questions, such as the consequences of poor timekeeping, is a good way of covering a lot of important topics in a short time (see Appendix 3.16, page 78).

4   Health and safety: students need to know that they are responsible for the health and safety of themselves *and others* while on work experience. They should be aware of the need to take sensible precautions, and identify first aid facilities and fire exits, from their first day. Most people do not really think about health and safety issues unless prompted, so it is a useful exercise to try and get them to envisage possible hazards in their placement firms. Obviously with vocational courses such as those for aspiring pharmacists or motor mechanics, there are likely to be uniform answers, but a mixed group of students should be able to come up with some very diverse ideas. The average office is rarely envisaged as a potential death-trap, but even there, trailing wires, overloaded filing cabinets and other detritus can take their toll. The Health and safety checklist (Appendix 3.3 on page 58) could also form the basis of a group discussion.

5   Racism and sexism: racist and sexist attitudes are sometimes encountered on work experience, but most tutors shy away from mentioning this, as they do not want to be seen as alarmist. You are doing students a disservice by failing to raise these issues. The majority of students are well aware that these problems may arise and some bold souls will introduce the topic themselves. Make sure that all students are familiar with the school/college's stance on these subjects and how it applies to them when on work experience. A suggested code of practice is given in Chapter 6 (Special Issues). Role play is probably the best way to deal with the issues raised here – either reading from a straight script, or improvising from an initial premise (see Appendix 3.15, Role Play Two, page 75). Racism, sexism and other facets of equal opportunities are dealt with in more detail in Chapter 6, which should provide plenty of additional material for case studies and role plays.

6   Enjoyment: finally, although much of this preparatory material seems to dwell on what can go wrong, stress that this is more a case of 'forewarned is forearmed'. The majority of students sail through their work experience without problems, so do emphasise this. It is meant to be an enjoyable as well as an educational exercise.

APPENDIX 3.1   A brief introduction for employers

NEWTOWN EDUCATION AUTHORITY

WORK EXPERIENCE

A brief introduction for employers

What is work experience?

- Work experience enables young people at school or college to spend short periods of time in a workplace gaining first-hand experience of the world of work.
- It is part of young people's education. They do not expect to be paid.
- The aim is to help young people understand what is expected of them at work, help them mature and enable them to present themselves more effectively for a permanent job.

Practical arrangements

- Virtually all pupils in Newtown do a work experience placement of two weeks, generally at age 15 years.
- Some have the opportunity to do a second placement when they are in the 6th form or at college.
- Second placements are often of three weeks, or sometimes on a one- or two-day per week basis throughout the year.
- Students normally come for a meeting with the employer before the placement.
- A teacher or lecturer normally visits the workplace during the placement to offer help and advice.
- Students on work experience are covered under the Health and Safety at Work Act.
- Newtown Authority has Personal Accident Insurance for all pupils on work experience. It also indemnifies employers against loss, damage, or injury during the placement (unless the employer is negligent).
- The Employeres' Liability Insurance generally covers pupils on work experience.
- Under the equal opportunities laws all placements must be made available to pupils regardless of their gender or race.

What can pupils actually do on work experience?

- The range of students' abilities and interests is very wide. At college and in the 6th form the range of courses which students follow is similarly very wide. Employers are simply asked to let us know the kinds of activities a young person might do in their workplace and we will match the placement with a suitable student.
- Students should behave and be treated as if they were in a real job.
- They normally work the same hours and accept the same disciplines as others in the workplace.

What exactly are employers expected to do?

- Employers are expected to offer the opportunity to do real work in a *safe* working environment.
- They should offer the supervision appropriate to young people having one of their first tastes of working life.

- They are not expected to be teachers or 'in loco parentis'.
- Employers are expected to behave as would a responsible and concerned adult.

Newtown Education Authority appreciates the contribution which employers can make to the education of young people through offering work experience.

If you would like to discuss this further, please contact:

The Work Experience Coordinator
Newtown Education Department,
3, Bridge St,
Newtown.

WITH THANKS FOR YOUR KIND INTEREST AND SUPPORT.

APPENDIX 3.2 Employers' notes for guidance

WORK EXPERIENCE

Many large organisations have well-structured 'induction' programmes for new staff, and a work experience pupil can slot into this or into a modified version of it. Smaller organisations do not always have the facilities to arrange such programmes. They may take on new or inexperienced staff so rarely that they have not had to consider such matters before.

This leaflet is intended for employers – large or small – and other staff in the workplace, simply as a guide to help you help the student make the most of the placement, and to help the placement run smoothly.

We emphasise that these are notes of guidance or advice only, designed to help the smooth running of the placement. We hope they will not entail extra work or appear burdensome to you.

Every workplace and employer is different – and of course every young person. We would not wish to prescribe exactly what is appropriate to your workplace.

Many of the points below will of course already have been covered by the teacher during the student's work experience preparation programme at school. Nevertheless, it helps for the employer to repeat and reinforce the same message.

The school is there at all times to support and advise you. Please do not hesitate to contact us.

Points for employers to cover with students at outset of work experience:

1 Remind students of the need to behave in a responsible way, and point out all possible risks, however small, connected with health and safety in the workplace.
2 Explain clearly procedures to be followed in the case of lateness or absence.
3 Ensure that pupils know any rules and regulations relating to the workplace, hours of work, etc.
4 It may be worth finding out a little about the student's domestic circumstances – college students' and school pupils' lives are not always organised around a normal working day. They may have younger brothers or sisters to collect from school, an evening job, a parent who needs an interpreter. It may be necessary to try to negotiate special arrangements to take account of these – wherever reasonable or possible – at your discretion. If such issues do present a problem, please contact the school or college straightaway.
5 Explain to all staff in the workplace why the student is there and what the purpose of the placement is. Try to gain their sympathy and support for the placement. Ill-informed staff can often have unrealistic expectations, and older staff may have forgotten how they felt when they first started work.
6 Ideally arrange for the student to be attached to an 'auntie' or 'uncle' figure – perhaps someone they will be working closely with to whom they can turn for advice and support. It may work better if the student is attached to someone near their own age, or a relatively junior member of staff. (This person could also help them complete the 'evaluation' at the end.)
7 Students are encouraged to deal with any problems in a mature and sensible way. They are encouraged to discuss problems or grievances in the first instance with the employer. We trust you will support us in this by listening sympathetically to students, if they do wish to talk things over with you. Again, never hesitate to contact the school if there is anything you cannot resolve.
8 Ensure that the student knows whom they should go to if there is anything they want to talk over.

9 Contact the school straightaway if you are unsure about anything, or if there are any unexplained absence or lateness. If a teacher needs to contact a pupil at home, or make a home visit, then the sooner we know the better.

10 Explain to the student in advance the kind of work schedule you have in mind for them. If there are any areas of negotiation, or possible flexibility, then explain this to the student.

For example, a shy or less able student may prefer to stay in one area, and work with the same people, for the whole period of the placement. The stress of a new environment and meeting new people may be challenge enough.

Other students may prefer to spend shorter amounts of time in different sections, for variety, stimulation and experience.

If you are able to offer this choice, or adapt as you go along, explain this to the student. We do, of course, appreciate that such choice is not always available, in which case this should be explained to the student.

11 Take the student round the workplace – or perhaps arrange for a junior member of staff to do so – on their first day, showing them where everything is and who everyone is. This will help to make them feel welcome, and at their ease.

12 Sometimes students are set assignments or projects to do around their placement.

This should not interfere with their doing their normal day's work unless by prior agreement with you.

We would ask, however, that you try to help the student wherever possible. For example, they may be asked to draw a plan of the organisation, to find out certain things about health and safety matters, or to interview a member of staff about career opportunities. Your cooperation is greatly appreciated.

13 Try to set aside a little time – it may only be 10–15 minutes – about half-way through the placement, when you can sit down with the student and discuss how things are going, and if any changes need to be made. Often young people will not voice their feelings unless encouraged to do so – especially in a new and strange place. This meeting can be instructive and helpful to all parties.

14 Finally, on the last day, or towards the end of the placement, try to find an opportunity to sit down with the student and discuss how the placement has gone. An 'evaluation form' is provided to help this process. Again, this can often be done quite effectively by a junior member of staff, and may be good experience for your staff, as well as for the student.

With thanks for your support.

APPENDIX 3.3   Health and safety checklist

Physical environment

Clean
Tidy
Good stacking/storage
Floorspace/exits clear
Clear demarcation of various activity areas
Dangerous substances stored separately/safely
Plenty of space

Machinery well maintained/safely positioned
Temperature
Ventilation
Noise level
Standard of conveniences, washing facilities,
   rest areas

Evidence of safety awareness

Safety policy displayed
Health and safety posters
First aid box
Named first-aiders
Accident book
Guards, goggles and protective clothing used

Who supplies protective clothing –
   student or employer?
Regular fire drills
Fire appliances – in evidence and accessible
Fire exits clearly marked

Attitudes to health and safety

Open discussion of health and safety issues
Awareness of legislation, responsibilities, etc
Existence of safety committee, etc
Safety training for staff
Identify possible hazards

Conscious of restrictions for trainees/students
Good supervision
Sympathetic attitude to needs of workers
List machinery and equipment students will use

Student induction and areas to be covered

Tour of building
Outline of health and safety policy,
   eg accident procedures

Explanation of conditions – hours, breaks, etc
Introduction to staff

APPENDIX 3.4   A placement description form

WORK EXPERIENCE
PLACEMENT DESCRIPTION

The information on this form will form part of a data base of placement information. It will be used to help teachers identify suitable students and to help students have realistic and informed expectations of the placement.

Name of organisation ....

Address ....

Contact .... Tel. no ....

Nature of business (including description of premises, number of staff or any other general information) ....

....

....

Description of placement   (Please give some examples of the kinds of activities a student might do on work experience) ....

....

....

Location/travel details   ....

Hours of work   ....

Facilities   eg canteen, staff bus ....

Any special requirements   (eg dress, specific skills) ....

Any other comments   ....

....

Would you kindly return this form to:*

        Work Experience Coordinator,
        High School,
        Newtown.

With very many thanks for your generous support and the trouble you have taken to complete this questionnaire.

* This section of the form is optional, see page 40.

Placement description form continued

Supplementary details*

1 Notes for teaching staff (eg will students work at locations other than on an employer's own premises, eg subcontractor's site, customer premises? Possibility of placements in other depts, languages spoken?)

2 Suitability for special-needs students (eg wheelchair access, nature of work):

3 Health and safety arrangements:

4 Union arrangements and attitude to work experience:

5 Insurance arrangements:

6 Equal opportunities policy:

---

* This section of the form is optional, see page 40.

APPENDIX 3.5   Confirmatory letter to employer (1)

(To confirm placement found by school or college where placement details have already been negotiated and agreed directly by the institution concerned)

_____

(Address)
Date as postmark

Dear

This letter is to confirm that student   will be coming to your organisation on work experience
from   to
A member of staff will be contacting you early in the placement to check on the student's progress and
to make arrangements for an informal visit.
Thank you for your help in arranging the placement: if you have any queries or need to contact me about
any aspect of the work experience, please do not hesitate to get in touch.

Yours sincerely,

_____

APPENDIX 3.6   Confirmatory letter to employer (2)

(To confirm placement initially offered by the employer to a centralised source, eg
LEA Work Experience Coordinator, and then passed on to the institution)

Newtown High School
Newtown.
(Date)

Dear

re: Work Experience Placements

Your name and telephone number, together with details of the placement(s) you may be willing to offer our students, have been passed to me by Newtown's Work Experience Coordinator. First may I thank you on behalf of the school and our students for your offer of work experience. I would like to confirm the following details:

Dates of placement:

Number of students I understand you are able to accept from the school during this period:

Number of places allocated to this school:

Name(s) of students I would like to place with you:

Contact name(s) and telephone number of teacher in charge:

I enclose CV(s) for the student(s) I would like to place with you. Would you be so kind as to complete and return the reply slip as quickly as possible, confirming (or otherwise) your willingness to accept this/these student(s).

If you would like to interview the student(s) prior to the placement would you indicate on the form and I will be glad to arrange an appointment.

Once I have received a reply slip from you confirming acceptance of this (these) student(s) (unless subject to interview) I will assume that the placement is firm and that no further action is required. The student(s) will simply arrive on the first morning at the agreed time.

If for any reason you subsequently have to withdraw the offer, would you be good enough to let me know as quickly as possible, so that alternative arrangements can be made. Similarly, if for any reason you are unable to confirm acceptance, would you let me know as quickly as possible.

We do prepare our students very carefully for their work experience and many are both nervous and excited. During the course of the placement a teacher will ring to arrange to visit you and the pupil at the workplace. The purpose of this visit is to monitor the progress of the placement and to give support and advice to you and to the student.

However, please do not hesitate to contact me if there are any difficulties whatsoever or anything you would simply like to talk over with me.

Once again, may I express my appreciation of the time and effort you are giving to our school and our students.

Yours sincerely,

_____

APPENDIX 3.7   Confirmation reply slip

WORK EXPERIENCE PLACEMENT
CONFIRMATION REPLY SLIP

Name(s) of student(s) ....

School/college ....

Dates of placement ....

I am able/unable* to confirm my acceptance of the above-named student(s) for work experience on the above dates, subject/not subject* to interview.

*Delete as appropriate.

On their first day they should report to:

.... (person),

at .... (address)

at .... (time)

Any comment ....

Name of organisation ....

Signed .... Date ....

Please return this reply slip to:

APPENDIX 3.8   Information for students

ALL YOU EVER WANTED TO KNOW ABOUT WORK EXPERIENCE
A STUDENTS' GUIDE

What is work experience?
A short period of 'placement' spent with an employer, which enables you to learn new skills and find out more about the world of work.

Do we have to do it?
Probably yes, as it is part of a policy made to ensure that all students gain some experience of working life. It may even count towards course work grades or Compact goals.

When is it and how long does it last?
The work experience dates are set at the beginning of the school year and you will be given this information as early as possible. Placements usually last two or three weeks.

What type of placements are available?
We shall be using all sorts of organisations and will try to place you in the sort of work which you prefer, although we can't guarantee your first choice.

What will it involve?
You will be given the same sort of duties and training as a new junior employee and will usually work normal business hours and follow the same routine as your colleagues.

Shall we be paid?
Sorry, no! With so many students going on work experience it would be impossible to find paid placements. But you will be able to claim back any extra travel expenses from the school. Details of how to claim will be given to you in due course.

What do we get out of it?
Hopefully, you will enjoy it and find out more about careers, training and life outside school. Some people obtain employer references and even permanent jobs as a result of work experience.

What if I'm unhappy or have problems?
You should let us know. We shall be in regular contact with the placement and a 'monitoring' tutor will be visiting to see how you are getting on.

What about equal opportunities?
We try to only use employers who offer equal work experience opportunities to all students. If you feel that this isn't the case, you should let the monitoring teacher know, so that we can try and sort things out.

And finally . . .
Most students enjoy their time on work experience, even though they may be nervous at first. It is valuable for their confidence and for future career and course choices.

APPENDIX 3.9   Formal application to coordinator for work experience

STUDENT'S CONFIDENTIAL APPLICATION FOR WORK EXPERIENCE

Name ....

Class/course ....

Home address ....

Date of birth .... tel ....

List in order of preference three types of work experience which interest you.

1. ....

2. ....

3. ....

Give details of any particular skills (acquired in or out of school/college) which may be useful on work experience, eg keyboarding, languages spoken. ....

....

Do you have any contacts who could provide work experience either for yourself or one of your classmates? Please write their names, addresses, and phone no. if possible: ....

....

Would you or your parents like to try and arrange your placement in the first instance? If so, please write down the names and addresses of your contacts here, and the kind of placement you have in mind: ....

....

Please give details of any public transport routes which you could use to travel to your placement, or any other transport available, eg lifts with parents: ....

....

Are there any health matters which may affect your placement or which the school or employer needs to be aware of? ....

....

Do you have any commitments which may affect your working hours when you are on your placement, eg a part-time job, domestic responsibilities? ....

....

Are there any other factors which might affect your placement, eg parental restrictions on travel, religious holidays, hospital appointments, etc? ....

....

Is there anything else at all that you think it would be helpful if the school or employer knows, eg you are particularly nervous, have never travelled alone before, you are looking forward to it, etc? ....

....

APPENDIX 3.10   Curriculum vitae

NAME	Lee Kempson
ADDRESS	3, Letsby Avenue, Rayndon RA2 1BC
TELEPHONE	Rayndon 987 6543
DATE OF BIRTH	16 March 1975
NATIONALITY	British

EDUCATION

1988–91, Rayndon Comprehensive School, Jeffries Lane, RA3 2DE
GCSE 1991
English Language(B), Art(B), French(C), Science(C), Maths(D)

1991 – date. St Oswald's College of F.E., Richston
BTEC National Diploma in Business Studies
(to be taken summer 1993)

WORK EXPERIENCE

November 1990. Two weeks' work experience at Hypeitt and Flogitt, estate agents. Duties included general office work, filing, photocopying, relief reception.
February 1991–date. Saturday and holiday work at Coots the Chemist, Richston. Duties include stocktaking, till work, customer service. I am now Assistant Supervisor in the Audio Dept.

INTERESTS

Athletics (member of Rayndon Harriers and represented school), member of college magazine committee, swimming, reading Science Fiction.

FURTHER INFORMATION

I have a long-standing interest in Law and have attended several sessions at Richston Crown Court. I am familiar with information technology, especially Amstrad and Apple Mac.

REFEREES

Ms C. Edwards, Course Tutor, Dept of Business Studies, St Oswald's College, Richston RC4 9EF
Mr Barry Lewis, Personnel Manager, Coots the Chemist, James St, Rayndon RA8 5GH

APPENDIX 3.11   A student's contract

STUDENT'S CONTRACT

Name of student ....

Name of organisation offering work experience

....

Address ....

....

1 I understand that work experience is part of my education and preparation for life and work.
2 I understand that work experience is temporary, unpaid and not intended to lead to a permanent job.
3 I agree to abide by company rules and regulations.
4 I agree to make every effort to deal with any problems in a mature and sensible way.
5 I understand that I am bound by the Health and Safety at Work Act and will act with consideration for my own safety and for the safety of others.
6 I agree to arrive on time, work the agreed hours and report all sickness and lateness according to the agreed procedure.
7 I agree to act with courtesy and consideration to fellow workers.
8 I understand that I should wear appropriate clothing.
9 I agree to complete my log book and any other assignments connected with the placement, to the best of my ability.

Signed .... Date ....

APPENDIX 3.12   Self-awareness questionnaire

1 What are your best subjects?

2 What are your worst subjects?

3 What skills do you have (eg good at making things, good at writing)?

4 What things do you think that you are not good at?

5 Give five words that best describe your personality

6 Below is a list of things which could happen on work experience. Number them in order of preference:

   meeting people
   working in a large firm/department
   chance to try out skills you already have
   only having a short journey from home to work
   working shift hours
   opportunity to acquire new skills

7 List five activities which you would like to do on work experience (eg use a computer, work outdoors)

8 List five activities which you would *not* like to do on work experience

9 Discuss your answers with a classmate or in a group. Do they agree with your self-assessment?

   What do your answers say about:
   (a) you as a person?

   (b) your choice of work experience?

APPENDIX 3.13 Interview *aide-mémoire*

STUDENT–EMPLOYER PRE-PLACEMENT *AIDE-MÉMOIRE*

This form is to be completed by the student in consultation with the employer.
It is intended to help employer and student ensure that all essential points are covered.

Name and address of employer ....

....

Name of student ....

Directions for getting there
On my first day I should go to:

....
(address if different from above).
Any directions for getting there (eg nearest bus stop) ....

I should arrive at .... (time) and report to .... (name of person).

Hours, breaks, etc
Normal time of arrival ....

Normal finishing time ....

Lunch break .... (times)

Other breaks (any arrangements) ....

Supervision
Name of person to whom I will be responsible: ....

If there are any problems I should discuss them with: ....

Names of people I will be working most closely with: ....

Health and safety
Any health and safety matters I should know about, which relate to this workplace: ....

....

Discipline
Any company rules which I should know about: ....

....

Dress
At my placement I should wear .... (any particular clothing).

Canteen or cooking facilities

....

Lateness

If I am forced to be late for a genuine reason, I should telephone .... (tel. no.).

I should ask to speak to (or leave a message for) .... (name).

I should always ring in before .... (time).

Note to students:

You should *always* say what time you *do* expect to arrive.

If you are unable to get to a phone yourself you should ask a parent, relative or friend to ring for you. Remember, lateness is not generally tolerated and may lead to dismissal, unless you have a *serious*, *genuine* reason.

Sickness

If I am *genuinely* sick and cannot come to work, I should telephone .... (tel. no.).

I should ask to speak to (or leave a message for) .... (name).

I should always ring in before .... (time).

Note to students:

You should always say when you *do* expect to return to work. Say a definite day. If you can't return on that day, you should ring again, following the above procedure.

Remember, employers generally use their discretion in deciding if reasons for absence are genuine. Giving reasons which the employer feels are not genuine can lead to dismissal.

If you do not want to go to work because you are unhappy for some reason, you should:

try and talk it over with the employer in the first instance, explaining why you are unhappy,

or

ring your teacher to talk it over,

and/or

talk it over with your parents.

Never just not turn up, or make excuses.

Any other information which the employer feels it is important for you to know:

....

....

....

Signed .... (employer) Date ....

Signed .... (student) Date ....

APPENDIX 3.14 Time-keeping

QUESTIONNAIRE

1 *Consequences*
What happens if the following people are late for work?

Doctor   Sales assistant
School caretaker   Actor
Airline pilot

2 *What would you do?*
Your colleagues on work experience are often a few minutes late getting back from break. Do you:

(a) follow their example – they are very friendly and you don't want to seem stand-offish?
(b) follow their example but explain to the supervisor why you were delayed?
(c) look at your watch and say that you think you'd better be getting back?

You're supposed to finish your work experience every day at five, but as you have to take the mail to the post office, you often don't get away until ten past. This means that you just miss a bus and have to wait 20 minutes. Do you:

(a) ask a work mate to do the job for you?
(b) phone your tutor and say that you're being exploited?
(c) explain the situation to your supervisor and ask if you can go to the post office five minutes earlier?
(d) do nothing – you don't want to cause trouble?

You have to leave home at 8 o'clock to get to work experience on time. This leaves you no time for breakfast. Do you:

(a) get to work at the right time and then have coffee and a biscuit while you are there?
(b) go hungry, but make sure that everyone knows it?
(c) have breakfast and get in late – you're only there for two weeks?
(d) get up earlier?

You're going to a pop concert which will mean leaving your work experience half an hour early. Do you:

(a) ask your supervisor if you can leave early just this once?
(b) just walk out at half-past four?
(c) ask your supervisor if you can leave early, but offer to make up the lost time?
(d) say you feel sick at lunch time and hope to be sent home?

3   *Time for thought*
Discuss the following statements about poor timekeeping:

It's OK once in a while   It means trouble for you
Everyone does it   It's rude and inconsiderate
It's the buses – they're always late   It's no big deal

APPENDIX 3.15   Role play exercises

In the role plays in the first section, two or three students can take part, but each should only be briefed about his or her own role. If you wish, the 'audience' can be told the full picture in advance. In the second section, students can improvise around the statements given *or* groups can 'brainstorm' their theories as to what might have led up to such a situation and how they would respond to it.

These exercises are a good way of illustrating the points in Chapter 3 (under 'Classroom preparation sessions') and of enabling students to try out techniques such as assertiveness. They also illustrate how various problems can sometimes be the result of ignorance and poor communications. The case studies outlined in other parts of the book can also be adapted in the same way.

Role Play One

You are the clerical supervisor in the Out Patients department of a large hospital. Your boss has asked you to have a work experience student for two weeks. You don't really know much about the student and why he's here. You don't want to give him anything too difficult to do in case he messes it up and causes more work for you. Anyway, you've just had to call him in to see you because the other staff have told you that he doesn't seem to be here half the time.

You are on work experience in a large hospital and you thought that you'd be getting experience on their computer system. But your supervisor treats you as if you were thick and all you are doing is filing. It's so boring that you've started to skive off, so now you've been asked to go and see the supervisor.

Role Play Two

You work in a small garage and a student from a local school is doing work experience there. The only thing is that she's a girl and you can't imagine why she would want to be a motor mechanic. You are enjoying teasing her by making remarks about women and you have brought in a pin-up calendar just to wind her up.

You are on a placement in a garage and you think that you can do the work well. But one of the young men there is really upsetting you by making sexist remarks. Now he's brought in a really tasteless calendar. You've had a few arguments with him already, but now you're really going to tell him what you think.

You are the boss of a garage and you have taken on a young woman for work experience. Her work is fine, but she is constantly having rows with Dave, your head mechanic. All he's doing is having a bit of harmless fun and you can't have her flying off the handle all the time. Perhaps she'd be happier in the office.

Role Play Three

You work in a busy pharmacy. You have a student on work experience, and you really haven't the time to be constantly supervising him. Other students who've been there on placement seem to have coped all right, but he seems unhappy, he doesn't do much and is very quiet. When his tutor comes to visit, you might suggest that he is moved elsewhere.

You really want to be a pharmacist and you were pleased to get this placement. But you're only doing a basic Science course at the moment and they are used to taking students who have quite an advanced knowledge of the subject. You think that you'd better explain the situation to your boss, but you're not terribly assertive and you don't want to be a bother to her when she's so busy.

Role Play Four

It is peak period in the travel agency which you run. A customer has complained about the way his travel arrangements have been handled. You suspect that he was dealt with by a work experience trainee, but you blame your chief clerk who should have been keeping an eye on him. You are going to have to call them both in to see what happened.

You are on placement in a travel agency. They allowed you to help arrange someone's holiday and you were sure that you could cope by yourself so you didn't bother to check details with Louise, the chief clerk. As a result you booked someone on to the wrong flight. Louise has barely spoken to you since, but you can't see why. It's not her problem is it?

You are the chief clerk in a travel agency. You thought that the work experience student seemed sensible, but he's totally messed up a customer's holiday because he couldn't be bothered to ask you how to use the computer booking system. He doesn't seem a bit sorry and you had to work overtime to get everything sorted out.

Role Play Five

You are the Personnel Manager in a record company and the last time you took someone on work experience they really worked hard. You offered them a job in the end. The young woman with you now is very pleasant, but isn't willing to put herself out. She enjoys all the perks, but last night when you asked her to stay late to finish an important job, she refused. This isn't the sort of industry where you can carry people who won't pull their weight, so you're going to ask her to finish at the end of this week. There are plenty of other students who want the placement.

You're having a fantastic time on your work experience at the record company. You've met some of the stars, been given tickets for concerts and everyone seems really friendly and easy going. Liz, the Personnel

Manager, was a bit put out when you couldn't stay late last night, but you're not being paid, after all. She's asked you to come and see her and you wonder if she's going to offer you a job like the last work experience student.

APPENDIX 3.16   'How dare you say that!'

Discuss or act out the following situations. What do you think led up to these remarks? What will happen next? How would you have handled it?

1 'In future, ask!'
2 'I'm not a Paki and you'd better watch what you say.'
3 'All you youngsters are the same. I don't know what they teach you nowadays. Half of you can't read and write.'
4 'Come on, love, smile. It was only a bit of a joke.'
5 'What's a lad like you doing here? I thought that nursing was a girl's job.'
6 'If you can't dress properly, don't come in tomorrow.'
7 'I'm not doing the photocopying. I'm taking A-levels you know.'
8 'Well, it's better than being Irish.'
9 'What's the matter? Are you stupid or something?'
10 'What time do you call this?'
11 'I do understand English you know.'

APPENDIX 3.17 Parent's letter for under-sixteens

Date

Dear Parent,

We are in the process of arranging work experience for your son/daughter, during the summer term.

The dates are:

The purpose of this letter is to explain the scheme and ask for your support.

The work experience scheme will involve your son/daughter spending two weeks in a real workplace gaining practical experience of the world of work. We have found that pupils of all abilities and interests can gain a great deal from this opportunity. They gain a better understanding of what is expected of them at work, which can help them when they eventually come to look for a permanent job. Just as important, they gain maturity, self-confidence and a sense of responsibility. As it is part of their education they do not expect to be paid. Their excess travelling costs will be met by the school. They will be expected to work the normal hours for their workplace. These are usually longer than a school day. If there is a genuine reason why this is not possible, then they should let us know well in advance and we will try to renegotiate the hours.

Free or subsidised lunches are available at some workplaces. Occasionally employers offer an allowance for lunch but they are under no obligation to do so. Where lunch is not provided students will have to pay for their own lunch or bring a packed lunch. Pupils eligible for free school meals will be able to claim a small allowance from the school. You should discuss this with the teacher responsible for work experience.

Pupils are sometimes nervous or apprehensive about work experience. They may also be excited and enthusiastic. Most thoroughly enjoy it once they get started.

Pupils will be asked to give a first, second and third choice of work placement. Every effort will be made to meet their requests but we cannot guarantee this. It should be emphasised that career sampling is not the main objective. The most important thing is the personal and social skills they gain, and the experience of the world of work.

All placements are vetted and pupils are fully covered by the LEA's insurance scheme. They will be visited at the workplace by a member of staff to check on their progress.

They are carefully prepared for their placement and given advice about health and safety and other matters. They may also be given course work to do connected with their placement.

You will be given the details of your son's/daughter's placement in due course.

Ms Taylor, who is responsible for the work experience programme, will be available at the 4th year parents' evening on .... if you would like to discuss the arrangements with her.

In the meantime we are working very hard in trying to find suitable placements. Your help would be very much appreciated. If you are able to suggest a suitable potential work placement – perhaps by asking

THE WORK EXPERIENCE MANUAL

at your own place of work or among your friends – this would be very helpful. It need not necessarily be for your own son/daughter. Could you write any contacts on the form below.

If you or your son/daughter wishes to arrange their own placement this is quite acceptable, but you must tell us so that we can check the placement, brief the employer and ensure that all the necessary paperwork is done.

We do hope you will give your full support to this scheme.

Finally, attached is a parent's contract/consent to work experience. Would you kindly sign it and return it by ....

Yours sincerely,

Ms Goodman,
Headteacher.

Suggestions for work placements:

Name & address of organisation ....

....

Name of contact .... tel ....

Nature of business/possible placement ....

....

Signed .... Date ....

APPENDIX 3.18   Parental consent form

PARENTAL CONSENT FORM

To the headteacher, St Benedict's School, and Oldshire Education Authority

I understand that as part of her/his education at the above named school, my daughter/son/ward .....

....

will be expected to make a number of education visits, some of which may be unsupervised. The visits will include going to industrial and commercial premises, in some cases undergoing practical work experience at the premises, and I give my consent.

Signature or responsible parent or guardian ....

Date ....

Address ....

....

APPENDIX 3.19   Contract form

PARENT/GUARDIAN'S CONTRACT

Name of student ....

Parent/Guardian's name ....

Name of organisation offering placement

....

Address ....

....

1 I understand that work experience is part of my son's/daughter's education and preparation for life and work.
2 I understand that the aims of work experience are:

   – to help my son/daughter better understand the demands and responsibilities of working life, and
   – to help him/her gain independence, responsibility and maturity.
3 I will cooperate in any way possible to help my son/daughter achieve these aims.
4 I understand that it is:

   – not necessarily job training,
   – not necessarily a trial period for a job,
   – not necessarily related to the kind of occupation or profession he/she eventually hopes to enter.
5 I understand that it is temporary and unpaid and not intended to lead to a permanent job.
6 I agree to give every encouragement and help to my son/daughter to make the most of the learning opportunity offered by work experience.
7 I agree to give every encouragement to my son/daughter to deal with any problems in a mature and sensible way, eg by encouraging him/her to discuss problems with me, with the supervisor at work, and/or with the teacher responsible for work experience.
8 I understand that my son/daughter will not be forced to remain in a placement which is clearly unsatisfactory, *provided reasonable efforts have been made to remedy any difficulties*.
9 I understand that pupils on work experience are bound by the Health and Safety at Work Act. I will encourage my son/daughter to act with consideration for the safety of him/herself and the safety of others.
10 I will make every effort to ensure that my son/daughter arrives on time at the workplace, works the agreed hours and reports sickness and lateness according to the agreed procedure.

Signed .... Date ....

APPENDIX 3.20   Letter to parent about placement

Date

Dear Parent,

I am pleased to be able to give you the details of your son's/daughter's work experience placement as follows:

Dates of placement ....

Name of organisation ....

Address ....

.... Tel ....

Contact name ....

Nature of business ....

Nature of placement ....

During the course of the placement your son/daughter will be visited by a teacher.

Name of visiting teacher ....

Name of teacher responsible for work experience ....

....

You are reminded that the employer as well as the school should be contacted immediately if your son/daughter is unable to attend the placement for any reason.

We do hope that your son/daughter will have a successful and enjoyable placement. Please give him/her your every support and encouragement, and please do not hesitate to contact me if you have any anxieties or queries.

Yours sincerely,

4

Monitoring progress during the placement

It is Friday afternoon. Your students have all been successfully placed and are due to start their work experience on Monday.

They have been prepared for their placement through a thorough, fully integrated, carefully planned, cross-curricular programme. They are highly motivated and eager in anticipation.

You have full parental support.

Your teaching colleagues share your enthusiasm for work experience and are keen to be involved in the monitoring. A programme of visits is pinned to the staffroom notice-board showing which member of staff is responsible for which student and placement – the result of close consultation with colleagues.

Your placements have been carefully selected and your employers and their staff fully briefed.

The matching of student to placement has been done meticulously.

You are pleased with yourself and quite rightly.

Now you've got them out – off the premises as it were. You're looking forward to a couple of weeks of peace, loads of free periods – a well earned rest. Right?

Wrong

The drama is only just unfolding!

If the placement is to run its course successfully, support needs to be given to the student, and to the employer and others in the workplace, in a planned and considered way.

Teaching staff may be apprehensive about contacting employers or resentful at having to give up their time to monitor placements. It is best to allow plenty of time for discussion and briefing of colleagues. Teachers who have had little to do with industry and commerce may feel nervous about visiting employers, or have their own stereotype of employers to deal with. They may need practical reassurance on a number of issues:

- If problems arise they may be the first point of contact, but need to know they have the backing of someone more experienced.
- If staff are familiar with a particular industry then try to allocate any placements in that industry to them. Allocating a visit to a hospital laboratory to a member of staff who doesn't know one end of a test tube from another may only add to their anxiety.
- Where possible, try to give staff placements which are near their own home or on their route home.
- Equip them with all the paperwork – placement description form, staff visit report form, interview *aide-mémoire* for staff (see Appendices 3.4, pages 59–60, 4.1, pages 92–3, and 4.2, page 94). Appendix 4.3 provides case study material that may be used for staff training on how to monitor work experience placements.

VISITING THE WORKPLACE DURING THE COURSE OF THE PLACEMENT

It is now virtually taken for granted that students should be visited at the workplace. We would suggest that the role of the person visiting should not be simply to carry out a one-off (or maybe two-off) visit, but that the 'visitor' should have a broader responsibility for the monitoring of the placement as a whole – a continuous responsibility which starts on 'day one' of the placement and continues through to the student's return to school or college at the end. This monitoring and support then becomes a whole process, equally as important as the preparation and debriefing.

It is important, therefore, that staff are clear about the purpose of the visit and the responsibility they carry.

Purpose of visit

To support the employer
Employers want, need, and are entitled to expect professional advice and support from the school or college which has placed its students into their charge.

Many employers do not have skills, confidence, expertise, and experience which many teachers have come to take for granted, ie in managing young people. Nor should we expect this.

Employers are generally concerned, often worried or anxious, to ensure that they are offering a worthwhile placement and the right kind of supervision and care.

They may find relating to shy pupils or coping with sullen or truculent ones quite a challenge.

The problems most often reported by employers – after those of attendance and punctuality – are to do with student shyness and communication difficulties in general.

Employers may perceive student apathy, absenteeism, or lateness as a rejection of themselves, their placement, workplace or industry. They may not realise that these things often spring from nervousness and misunderstandings. This sense of rejection can quickly turn to anger, especially if they feel they have taken trouble to devise a worthwhile placement.

Most employers welcome and appreciate regular contact with the school and a visit from the student's teacher.

They may well be looking forward to the teacher's visit, in order to have someone with whom to talk over the placement and to seek support and reassurance.

They may be delighted with the student's progress and performance, perhaps becoming more aware of some of the prejudices they held before the placement, for example, about ethnicity or gender, or about a particular school or area. They often find the liveliness and open-naturedness of young people surprising and refreshing. They value the opportunity to express and communicate their positive perceptions as well as the negative ones.

They can feel disappointed or aggrieved not to have this opportunity. They may wonder why they went to so much trouble over the placement if the teacher does not then show an interest. Even if there are no real difficulties, employers may feel that failure to visit is discourteous and shows lack of interest on the teacher's part. They may be less inclined to offer work experience in future.

Without this support and active interest, their continued support and future cooperation may be jeopardised. Where employers do have grievances or frustrations which have not been properly acknowledged and taken on board by the school, they will often simply vote with their feet and withdraw their support – perhaps offering fewer or no placements in future, and asking to be given a rest from students for a while! Others simply offer excuses for not taking students, feeling it is just not worth the trouble.

Work experience involves a great deal of time and effort from those in the workplace. Only the most committed and conscientious employers will take the trouble to initiate discussion with you, or articulate their concerns. Many will not even have given a great deal of consideration to the matter. Why should they? Attending to the needs of young people is not after all their principal *raison d'être*. They may simply be left with a vague feeling that work experience is just a lot of aggravation for them.

To support the student

Most students, like employers, expect and welcome a visit from a member of the teaching staff. Ideally this should be the person who arranged the placement in the first place, or at least someone who knows the student. However, one must recognise that this is not always possible. Whoever it is, it is important that the visitor is clear about the reasons for the visit and how to conduct the visit.

A work experience placement, by its very nature, is not, nor is intended to be, a training or teaching environment. The relationships of the workplace are different from those of school or college, and the pupil–teacher relationship is, in some respects, a difficult and awkward one, in this situation.

Relating to a student on a one-to-one basis requires a different set of skills from those needed in the classroom.

Below are some common observations made by students about the 'visit':

– 'Work experience was a taste of adult life. I was treated like an adult and enjoyed this aspect of it. The arrival of a teacher threw me back into the role of pupil, and made me feel like a child again – in front of colleagues in the workplace.'

- 'The teacher failed to turn up for a visit. I felt let down.'
- 'I felt cheated. The teacher spent ages with the employer and only a short time with me.'
- 'I felt embarrassed by the teacher's visit. It drew attention to me.'

Students often feel particularly embarrassed by inappropriate dress or behaviour on the part of the teacher:

- 'I was working in a bank and the manager there was quite old-fashioned. Female staff have to wear tights no matter how hot the weather and men have to wear shirts and ties. They'd just had a bit of a scourge on "standards of dress" the week before. You can imagine how I felt when the teacher turned up in a short skirt and t-shirt.'

On the other hand students often feel quite proud of showing off their new skills and relationships they have made. They are delighted to go into detail about activities of which their tutors are ignorant and in which they have gained some experience.

In summary then, the visit has the following purposes:

1   To *check* the suitability of the work and workplace.
2   The *supervision* of the student – to monitor the performance and behaviour of the student.
3   To show *concern* and give *support* to the student.
4   To demonstrate the *importance* of work experience and show that it is being taken seriously.
5   To *resolve any difficulties* – act as mediator, help the student cope with problems and to intervene yourself if necessary.

Carrying out the visit – what to do/what not to do

The sections below, 'Setting up the visit' and 'Carrying out the visit', describe the practical steps which can be taken, and points to note, which will enable you to help the employers offer a more worthwhile placement and ensure their continued commitment, and to help the student maximise the potential of the placement as a learning experience.

Setting up the visit
Telephone the employer within the first few days to:

1   Check the pupil is there.
2   Pick up on any problems early, before they get out of hand. This will enable you to schedule an early visit to those placements where there is evidence of greater need.
3   Show the employer and student that you are taking an active interest and concern right from the start.
4   Reinforce and repeat to employers that they should report absenteeism early, and should not hestitate to contact you if they have any concerns they wish to talk over. If you don't know about problems until the last week of the placement, there is not much you can do about them by that stage.
5   Arrange an appointment to visit. It will be advisable to explain:

   - What the purpose of the visit is. It is important that neither student nor employer feels threatened. Both should see this as supportive to them.

- What the format of the visit is – namely, that you think it would be useful to talk to both the student, and their immediate supervisor, separately. Explain why.
- Ask if there is anyone else (eg a section supervisor, or another manager) with whom it would be important or useful for you to talk.
- How long you expect the visit to take, and how long you anticipate spending with each party – the employer and the student. This needn't be very long but it is good that employers are warned. It may mean they arrange for someone else to cover the shop for 10 or 15 minutes while they talk to you, and that they won't need to keep popping in and out. Also it may reassure them to know that you don't anticipate spending half the morning with them. You don't, of course, need to be rigid about this – when you get there you'll judge the situation.
- That you would appreciate the opportunity to talk to the student in private and ask if this will be possible. This will give the employer the chance to make any necessary arrangements.

Since you will have to ring *anyway* to arrange a visit, this preliminary telephone call should not entail extra work. The point is simply that it should be made earlier rather than later. It may prevent a crisis. It will hopefully make the actual visit more worth while.

Carrying out the visit
Dress smartly. In many workplaces casual dress is not acceptable.

In general, take a form to complete. It looks professional as well as providing you with a useful *aide-mémoire*. It shows you are listening carefully and are concerned and interested. The sample staff visit report form shown in Appendix 4.1 (pages 92–3) may be used as a checklist of points to cover and questions to ask.

There may be instances where note taking or form completing could appear threatening to the employer or student, or inappropriate for other reasons. It may be a reassuring courtesy in any event to ask if the student or employer minds if you complete the form. You might explain what the form is about and complete it together with the student or employer. This will give a focus and structure to your discussion. Or you may simply complete it afterwards. You will need to assess the situation and make a judgement.

In any event the three key points here still stand:

1   Show that you regard work experience as important and that you are concerned.
2   Be clear about the points you wish to cover with both the student and employer.
3   Ensure that the employer and student have been given full opportunity to express their concerns.

Don't overrun the time allowed and agreed, unless it is with the express permission of the employer or it is quite clear the employer wants to talk.

Your job is primarily to elicit information, listen, and draw out both employer and student.

Let us now look, in more detail, at how this can be achieved, in respect of the student. The following is a list of 'prompter' questions, to give some ideas to the visitor on what may be appropriate to ask. This section can be read in conjunction with Appendix 4.1 mentioned above.

1   *Checking the suitability of the work and workplace*
It is important here to refer also to Chapter 6 on 'Special issues' – specifically equal opportunities and health and safety matters.

Remember, the object is to draw out the student, encouraging him/her to talk. Some ways of drawing out the student are:

- Ask the student to *describe* the work s/he is doing.
- Ask about the *level* of difficulty – is it too demanding/stressful/difficult/easy/boring?
- Ask about the level of *responsibility* they have. Would they welcome more? Could they cope with more? Is it about right?
- Ask how *structured* the work is. Do they have a programme to work to? Are they given tasks, as and when they come up? Are they expected to just get on with things which need doing without being asked? Which way do they prefer?
- Ask how *varied* the work is. Do they work in more than one department? Would they prefer to move around or stay in one department? Are there any jobs or departments they would like the opportunity to sample? Would they prefer to stay in one place and get to know the job and people better?
- Ask how they are getting on with *assignments* or *diaries*. Do they need help? Is there any way in which the people in the workplace could help them? Have they the confidence to ask?
- Are they *maximising the opportunity* available to them? Have they had the chance to ask questions about career opportunities/entry requirements/how people came to be doing the jobs they are doing?

2   *Supervision of the student – performance, reliability, punctuality, attendance*

- Ask about the student's *domestic circumstances*. Are there any circumstances which may affect the student's performance, attendance or punctuality?
- Are there children to collect from nursery or school? Other dependent relatives?
- Is there a parent with a limited command of English who relies on the student as an interpreter?
- Domestic arrangements may be organised around school or college hours, and not around the workplace hours. Work experience can disrupt a carefully worked out routine.
- It may be unreasonable to expect family commitments to be disrupted for a two- or three-week placement.
- Ask about *other factors* which can affect a student's ability to perform well on work experience.
- Do they have an *evening job*?
- Do they have to help in the *family business* in the evenings?
- Do they have to prepare the family's *evening meal*?
- Do they have a particularly *difficult journey*?

3   *Support of student*
It is particularly important here to ensure that the student is given every opportunity to express anxieties, views, etc.

- Ask the student about *relationships* in the workplace.
- To whom does s/he report? Is that person approachable? Is that person accessible/available/

interested/not interested?
- Ask about *others in the workplace.*
- Is there anyone else the student feels is particularly helpful?
- Is there anyone who makes them feel unwelcome?
- Do people understand why the student is there?
- Have there been any misunderstandings?

4   *Resolving difficulties*

There may be problems the student wishes to talk over with you – problems which s/he has felt unable to discuss with the workplace supervisor, or deal with her/himself.

In the first instance it may be enough to allow the student to air the problem with you. No action may be necessary. In any event you should discuss any proposed action with the student first. Don't assume that the student necessarily wants action. S/he may feel it adequate that s/he has voiced any concerns. The student may indeed prefer to put up with things rather than cause a fuss. Acting hastily could simply embarrass the student.

If action is needed, then it may be more appropriate that the student her/himself takes it. Learning to cope, and deal with problems in a mature and constructive way, is, after all, part of the exercise. All that is then required of you in this situation is that you help the student to be clear about how they should deal with it and have the courage to do so. It may be simply a question of the student asking the employer for a transfer to another section, or for the opportunity to vary the workload, or try something new.

There may, however, be instances where you feel it necessary to play the role of mediator, perhaps voicing the concerns of the student to the employer, or vice versa, or perhaps setting up a three-way discussion.

Finally you may decide to set an early date for a subsequent meeting. Make sure that both employer and student feel encouraged to contact you if needed.

Supporting the employer – 'prompt' questions

This section of the staff visit report form (see Appendix 4.1) has deliberately been kept shorter and more general than the section which relates to the interview with the student. This is not meant to inhibit discussion or imply that less time need necessarily be spent with the employer. It is simply a recognition that employers may have less time to spare than the student and that this needs to be respected and acknowledged.

However, some prompter questions might be:

- Is the employer satisfied with the student's punctuality and attendance?
- Is the employer satisfied with the student's interest and motivation?
- Does the employer feel the student's ability matches the work s/he is able to offer?
- How is the student fitting in with the other staff?
- Is there anything you can do to help the employer offer a better placement?
- Is there anything you can do to help the employer cope with the student?
- Is there anything you can do to help the student benefit more fully from the opportunity offered?

- Has the student approached the employer for help with diary completion or assignments?
- How has the employer felt about this?

Ultimately, it should be remembered, the employer always has the right to insist on the immediate withdrawal of the student.

Also, little is achieved by ordering the student to complete a placement (see Case Study 5, page 132).

If a placement does not meet the needs of one student, there may be other students who would find it worthwhile. It is rarely worth jeopardising a good relationship with an employer, and depriving future students of the opportunity to use that placement.

Also, as we have been, employers need support and advice, and many 'difficult' employers, with support and experience, can still offer worthwhile placements.

If you do feel that the best course of action is simply to withdraw the student, it is always best that this should be done with little animosity, greatest understanding, and after every effort has been made to resolve or improve the situation.

The student also needs to know, and to have the reassurance that you *are* prepared ultimately simply to withdraw him/her, but only after all methods of making the placement work have been explored.

APPENDIX 4.1   Staff visit report form

WORK EXPERIENCE – STAFF VISIT REPORT FORM

Name of student ....

School/college/course ....

Placement name & address ....

....

Student's supervisor at placement ....

INTERVIEW WITH STUDENT

General
What are the student's overall feelings about the placement? Comment/describe.

Work
What work is the student doing? Comment/describe.

Has the student completed any practical or written work which s/he can show you and/or keep at the end of the placement? Describe.

How does the student feel s/he is coping with the level of work? Too difficult? Too easy? Describe.

Does the student feel s/he has enough tasks to fill the day? Is s/he bored? Under too much pressure? Comment.

Relationships with other staff
How does the student feel about the other staff? Does s/he find them friendly/unfriendly? Helpful/unhelpful? Comment.

If there are problems, what attempt has the student made to deal with them him/herself?

Supervision/care
Are there any circumstances which could affect the student's performance, attendance or punctuality? Comment.

Personal problems?

Domestic circumstances?

Travelling difficulties?

Financial?

Any other?

MONITORING PROGRESS DURING THE PLACEMENT

If there are problems, then, with the student's permission, have the employer or other staff been made aware of these? Comment.

Is the student quite clear with whom s/he should discuss problems, report difficulties, absences, etc?

Does the student feel confident/happy about approaching this individual?

INTERVIEW WITH EMPLOYER

General
What are the employer's overall impressions of the student? His/her attitude to placement, etc?

Does the employer have any worries or concerns about the student's general welfare?

Work
Is the employer satisfied with the student's performance, ability, effort?

Are there any aspects of the work which the employer feels the student is having difficulty coping with?

Does the employer feel that the student has shown any special areas of strength or particular success?

Relationships
How does the employer feel the student is fitting in with the other staff?

Is the employer aware of any stresses, potential or actual sources of conflict or misunderstandings?

Supervision/care
Is the employer satisfied with the student's punctuality/attendance?

GENERAL

Comment on working conditions/general environment?

Comment on attitude of employer/other staff to student?

Signature .... Date ....

SUBSEQUENT VISITS

Comment	Signature	Date

APPENDIX 4.2 *Aide-mémoire* for staff

AIDE-MÉMOIRE FOR STAFF RESPONSIBLE FOR MONITORING WORK EXPERIENCE PLACEMENTS

- You are responsible for the ongoing support of the student and the employer throughout the course of the placement, principally to offer support, advice and reassurance wherever needed.
- Phone the employer on the first day of the placement. Introduce yourself, check the student is there and ask if there is anything the employer wishes to discuss, or any anticipated problems.
  Make a definite appointment to visit. Ask that the student is informed of the date and time of the visit.
- You may not be able to reach the employer when you first phone and it is not always possible for him/her to get back to you. Keep trying!
- Don't visit without warning. It could be inconvenient or disruptive or you may find the employer or student is not there.
- If you are delayed or unable to visit at the arranged time, let the employer know.
- Dress smartly. Casual dress is acceptable in some workplaces but it is best to err on the cautious side.
- Wherever possible, try to speak to the student and employer separately and in private.
- Again, ideally try to have your chat with the student first. Whichever party you see first, report back to the other before you leave.
- Don't just breeze in and out! Most students and employers see this visit as important and helpful. Don't overstay your welcome either. They have work to do. (So do you, no doubt!)
- Use the staff visit report form as a prompt for covering all relevant questions.
- Suggest a subsequent visit or phone call if this seems necessary, ie if there are signs of problems developing. Invite them to contact you if they need help.
- If there are any difficulties you don't feel you can sort out yourself, then let .... know as soon as possible.

APPENDIX 4.3   In-service materials for staff training

The following case studies are intended to be used as part of an in-service training programme for those members of teaching staff who will be responsible for monitoring the placement.

Staff may be asked to work in small groups to look at the case studies and consider the following questions:

1 What factors might contribute to the success of this placement?
2 What do you think are the expectations, hopes, and/or anxieties of the employer or pupil (as appropriate) in relation to the teacher visit?
3 What would your role as teacher be in relation to the employer or pupil (as appropriate)?
4 How can you facilitate the success of the placement?
5 How can you ensure the continued support of this employer? (Placements are in short supply.)

The case studies and questions are designed to help teaching staff empathise with employers, and with pupils (whose expectations and perceptions of teachers may be different from those they held at school or college), focus the minds of teaching staff on the needs of employers and students and break down some of the stereotypes or misconceptions some teachers may hold about employers.

Staff might be asked to feed back their perceptions to the larger group as a whole. This may then lead into a discussion or further exercise where teachers are asked to identify and prioritise the aims and objectives of a monitoring visit.

Case studies 1 and 3 are linked – in that Case study 1 describes the employer's perspective on the placement and Case study 3 describes the same placement from the pupil's point of view. Case studies 2 and 4 are linked in the same way. For the purposes of the exercise it's probably better if the small groups don't see the other case studies until the whole group comes together to give its responses at the plenary session at the end.

At the end of the case studies are some possible responses to them.

Case study 1 – employer
You are a 25-year-old assistant administration manager in a large insurance company. You left school at 16 and have never looked back. Your area manager has persuaded you that it would be a good thing to have a pupil from a local school in your department for work experience. Although you can see it is a good idea and agree that big companies should 'do their bit', you are not very keen at first as the school concerned had a 'bit of a reputation' in your day. In the event, the girl placed with you has turned out much better than you expected – more outgoing and brighter. You're worried that the work you're giving her might be a bit boring for her but you can't think of anything else to give her to do and you're terribly rushed yourself and haven't really had time to think about it. Her teacher is coming next week to monitor the progress of the placement. You are rather concerned about the impending visit.

Case study 2 – employer
You are the 50-year-old owner/manager of a small garage. You have agreed to take a pupil on work experience. You think it's a wonderful idea and you wish they'd done 'that sort of thing' in your day. You're trying to give the pupil as much variety as possible and some of the more interesting jobs – ie really teach him something. However, he seems half asleep most of the time, does everything wrong, and can't seem to remember what he's told from one minute to the next. He turns up late in the morning, and once

didn't turn up at all. This makes it impossible to organise the day's work. He says he wants to go to college to learn motor mechanics . . . but honestly you wonder what they teach them in school these days. His teacher is coming next week. The teacher said something about 'checking the suitability of the placement'. You are rather concerned about the impending visit.

Case study 3 – pupil

You are placed for work experience in a large insurance company. You are enjoying the novelty of the new environment and have made some new friends. You feel you can cope well with the work you are being given. Others depend on your doing your job well and this makes you responsible and adult.

Your teacher is coming to see you next week. You haven't had much time to do your diary and you haven't even started any of the assignments.

Case study 4 – pupil

You are placed in a small garage. You're really keen to do the placement as you hope it will help you get a place on a motor mechanics course at college. A teacher is coming to see you next week. You don't want to admit that the work is harder than you expected. Furthermore, the boss is on your back just because you were half an hour late. You can't see why he's making such a fuss and anyway it wasn't your fault. You have a part-time job in the evenings and you keep arriving there late, too, because of your placement.

Some possible responses

Case study 1

Factors contributing to success of placement:

- Initial enthusiasm on part of employer for the idea of taking a young person for work experience.
- Motivated by idea that large employers should 'do their bit' (for education/young people) rather than simply self-interest.
- Positive perception of young person on placement.
- Some of employer's prejudices about the school the girl has come from already challenged.
- Employer genuinely concerned to give pupil a worthwhile experience (not wanting to just use her).

Possible expectations, hopes, anxieties of employer:

- Left school at age 16 and 'never looked back' – some relief at leaving school? Doesn't wish to be reminded of school? Possibly some lingering tensions with respect to relationship with teacher?
- Fear that teacher has come to check up on her – feeling guilty that she isn't doing enough for pupil? Anxieties about whether placement is worthwhile or suited to pupil's needs?
- Worried about how much time visit will take. (She's obviously under pressure herself and anxious about her own workload.)

Role of teacher in relation to employer:

- To offer reasssurance, support and advice.

How might teachers facilitate success of placement/ensure continued support of employer?

- Give encouragement and support to employer – thank employer. Given initial enthusiasm and genuine concern for pupil, some positive encouragement to employer might help to motivate the employer in relation to the pupil.
- Use opportunity to find out how pupil feels about placement and feed this back to employer – do not

assume that employer's perceptions are same as pupils until you have listened carefully to both parties.
- Explain clearly purpose of visit when phoning to arrange visit – reassure that purpose of visit is to offer help and advice.
- Give some indication of how long visit will take.
- Discuss with both employer and pupil appropriateness of placement and any changes possible or necessary.

Case study 2

Factors contributing to success of placement:

- Employer's enthusiasm for scheme.
- Employer genuinely trying to give pupil stimulating, interesting and varied placement – making a real effort.

Possible expectations/hopes/anxieties of employer in relation to teacher visit:

- Is feeling frustrated with pupil at this stage – rather than angry – hopes perhaps for teacher to 'knock some sense into pupil' – or get to the bottom of why he appears so demotivated.
- Hopes to discuss suitability of pupil's career aspirations with teacher – wonders whether this is the right placement for him? As someone experienced in the field, he expects to have his views on this considered seriously.
- Perhaps hoping to have the opportunity to 'have a go' at the education system?
- Is worried that teacher is coming to check up on his garage, the way he runs his business – perhaps feels affronted by this?

Role of teacher in relation to employer:

- Need to explain purpose of visit in a way which doesn't put employer on the defensive or make him feel threatened.
- Need for tact and sensitivity in dealing with employer – and respect for his experience and expertise in his field.
- Need to show some appreciation of the effort he has put into the placement on behalf of the pupil.
- Need to find out from pupil his feelings about the placement – why he is late so often – why he appears half asleep – don't jump to any conclusions until you've listened to all parties.

How to facilitate success of placement/ensure continued support of employer?

- Need to acknowledge effort made by employer.
- Listen to both pupil and employer.
- May be especially important in this instance to talk to pupil in private as you need to tackle the issue of time-keeping and attitude – but also elicit from him if there are genuine reasons for lateness/ tiredness, or any anxieties he has about the work.
- Indicate to both parties that you are prepared to withdraw the pupil from the placement if necessary but that you wish to make sure you have tried every way possible of remedying the situation first – get employer's support in this.

Case study 3

Factors contributing to success:

- Pupil clearly enjoying placement – work stimulating enough in the short run – the novelty of the new environment, new friends, and new responsibilities, sufficient to make the placement worth while – the feeling that she can cope well with the work.

Expectations/hopes/anxieties of pupil in relation to teacher visit:

- Worrying about assignments and diary – teacher visit causing stress – how important is the diary in relation to what she is getting out of the placement?
- Feeling 'adult and responsible' – perhaps fear teacher will make her feel less so in front of new-made friends?
- Feeling she is doing her job well – is fully stretched – hopes she will not have workload changed as a result of the visit?
- Perhaps hopes for opportunity to show off new skills, responsibilities and adult status to teacher?

Role of teacher in relation to pupil:

- To be supportive and give encouragement.
- Take active interest in work pupil is doing – ask pupil to show her round, explain the work of the department, and her own work.
- Ask what help or advice she needs in completing assignments or diaries.
- Perhaps bring employer and pupil together to see how pupil can be helped to complete assignments – perhaps other members of staff would be willing to help?

How to facilitate success of placement/ensure continued support of employer:

- See all of above!

Case study 4

Factors contributing to success of placement:

- Pupil very keen and committed – sees this as an important stepping-stone in career aspirations.
- Is aware of poor time-keeping – seems to be concerned and possibly is trying?

Role of teacher in relation to pupil:

- Clearly important to elicit reasons for lateness from pupil and draw to his attention that the employer says he seems tired all the time. Is he tired?
- Important to talk to pupil on his own as he may not be willing to discuss this in front of employer.
- Important here to gain pupil's confidence and assure him that while the employer has some misgivings you and he are still prepared to give him a chance.
- Important to elicit information about part-time job – clearly pupil is finding it difficult to juggle this and the placement – possibly it's keeping him up late and this is reason for tiredness?
- Is level and volume of work appropriate? Can he cope? Need to gain pupil's trust if pupil is to be honest?

How to facilitate continued success of placement:

- Talk to employer about pupil's circumstances – part-time job possibly involving working fairly late in the evening. Is the money he earns in his part-time job important to him and to his family? Employer may be more sympathetic if he understands pupil's circumstances. Possible adjustment of pupil's hours of work could be negotiated so that he's not constantly late arriving at both his part-time job and to his work experience placement?

- Talk to employer about pupil's career aspirations and how important placement is to him. Again, employer may be more synmpathetic.
- Possibly employer has overestimated pupil's abilities – has unrealistic expectations of him? After all it's a long time since he was an apprentice and he's probably come to take a lot for granted? Also it's only a small garage so he may not have recruited inexperienced staff for a very long time. Possibly his attempts to give pupil a varied workload are not appropriate – some more straightforward jobs might be more suitable for this pupil?

Some general points

Clearly any of the above scenarios could so easily have developed into problems, not necessarily of anyone's making, simply the result of lack of communication and wrong assumptions. With careful and supportive monitoring, however, they all have the potential to become really successful placements.

We hope that discussions around the above case studies will highlight some of the key factors crucial to a successful monitoring visit:

- Importance of setting it up properly. Explaining purpose, so that all parties perceive the visit as supportive rather than threatening.
- Importance of talking to both parties (and others in the workplace where appropriate) in private and apart from each other. Again, the reason for this needs carefully explaining.
- And most importantly of all – the need for good listening skills, the ability to draw out the concerns of pupil and employer.

5

Debriefing

In the debriefing exercise there are – as with all other aspects of the management of work experience – broadly three groups whose needs have to be met: the employer (and employees) without whom none of this would be possible; the student, without whom none of it would be necessary, and finally the teacher and colleagues whose continued willingness to experience the martyrdom of work experience organisation needs to be assured!

DEBRIEFING THE STUDENT

Debriefing the student has the following purpose:

– to exploit to the full the placement as learning experience by:

1 Allowing the student to reflect on the experience and draw from it important lessons, eg about handling situations and relationships.
2 Allowing the student to consider what s/he has learnt about the world of work in general.
3 Increasing the student's knowledge of occupations, workplaces and careers, through the pooling of information and experiences in discussions with other students, etc.
4 Enabling the student to consider how this learning can assist him/her in applying for a job, in improving interview skills, etc.

Some of the above can be achieved by the student acting individually, eg completing the self-appraisal form (Appendix 5.2, page 108) and the review of placement form (Appendix 5.3, page 109). However, many of the above learning-points only become realised when the student is sharing his/her experience with that of other students, or through discussion with other individuals, such as the employer.

The following activities have been successfully used as part of a debriefing exercise:

– One-to-one, or small group discussions at the workplace between the student, the supervisor and/or others at the workplace. This kind of activity needs to be part of a process of ongoing appraisal and support offered by the employer. The school will need to offer appropriate encouragement and support to the employer, eg through the provision of materials (see the employer's open report in Appendix 5.1, page 107), and through *quality* monitoring visits and general support. The process should start with the workplace induction and culminate in the last-day 'review'. (This is discussed in more detail below in the section dealing with the employer's debriefing.)

- Student's self-appraisal and review of placement forms (Appendices 5.2 and 5.3, on pages 108 and 109).
- Completion of assignments built around the placements.
- Verbal feedback in a structured way to other students in small groups, eg students are each asked to do brief prepared presentations. Groups can be led by an invited employer, 'adults-other-than-teachers' or by teaching staff. (Feedback can be by video.)
- Students may be 'paired off' to interview each other.
- Students may work on their own, in pairs or in small groups to mount displays about their work experience, eg descriptions of work, workplace, photographs taken at workplace, samples of firm's brochures, promotional materials, staff rotas and other 'take-away' materials which give a flavour of the workplace, transcripts of interviews conducted at the workplace, etc.
- Students may make a video describing their experience, eg interviewing each other.
- Video may be made at the workplace, say of interviews with members of staff at the workplace.
- Members of school staff and other interested parties may be invited to view and participate in student debriefing.
- Students may write thank you letters to employers as part of, for example, English course work. They are encouraged to give employers full and constructive comments on what they got out of the placement, rather than a perfunctory standard letter. (See section below on employers' needs with respect to debriefing.) Letters may also include an invitation to 'open day', 'buffet lunch' or simply to view debriefing materials on display at school. (See Appendix 5.4, page 110.)
- Students may be presented with a work experience certificate like the one in Appendix 5.8, page 116, to round-off the placement and promote a sense of achievement.
- Participation in the organisation of an open day or similar event aimed at employers. The organisation of such an event and students' involvement in it becomes an extension of the learning experience of the placement and worth while in itself.
- Wherever appropriate, students may write to employers a few months later to keep them informed of their progress. They could also use the opportunity to remind employers that next year's group will also be needing placements and urge them to consider taking students again. (See Appendix 5.5, page 112.)

These latter two exercises, as well as being valid exercises in themselves, also help to 'promote' work experience to employers. Students themselves are – can be – the best adverts for work experience. Try to use every resource you have to its maximum advantage.

DEBRIEFING PARENTS

We have earlier stressed the importance of involving parents in the preparation for work experience, so it would be cavalier to exclude them from the debriefing process. They will want to know what their child did on the placement and how he or she progressed – and pupils themselves may not always be forthcoming with accurate information or any information at all.

Work experience reports are, in theory, confidential, although students and parents can ask to see them, but parents should always be sent a resumé of what their son/daughter has achieved on work experience. This need not involve extra work, it could be the employer's open report, which is discussed opposite (see also Appendix 5.1, page 107), or the student's own self-assessment of the placement, perhaps with brief tutor comments. Alternatively, many pupils will include details of their work experience in their records of achievement and the existence of such documents can be drawn to parents' attention, or the relevant pages sent to them. Don't forget that once a student is over compulsory school age, his or her consent is necessary before doing any of the above.

Feedback can be given to parents in other ways too: an overview of the work experience in newsletters, school magazines, presentations/exhibitions, at parents' evenings and open days and availability of tutors to discuss placements at same. Parents also often attend careers interviews with their offspring and hopefully the careers officer will have been briefed about the work experience and be able to discuss its relevance with both parties. Where appropriate, it should also be mentioned in the action plan drawn up at the end of the careers consultation. Students do show these action plans to parents not able to be present at interview.

In short, parents should see work experience as just as much part of the curriculum as science or languages and be appraised of their child's progress as they would be for formal subjects.

DEBRIEFING THE EMPLOYER

The debriefing of employers has two broad purposes:

1   To use the employer as a valuable resource in the debriefing of the student.
2   To offer the employer the opportunity to express views and receive feedback and support from the school and student.

The employer's role in debriefing student(s)

Apart from meeting employers' own legitimate needs and demands, the employer's feedback and involvement in the debriefing is central to the benefit which the student derives from the placement.

The employer's report on the student – whether good or bad – *can* be a valuable learning experience for the student. A good report can boost the student's confidence and provide a valuable asset in job hunting. Sometimes students whose performance or behaviour at school leaves much to be desired nevertheless perform well on work experience. A good reference from a work experience employer may be one of the few positive documents with which the student – especially a poor attender – leaves school. In any event an employer reference should never be undervalued. Employers often will take more notice of what another employer says than of a teacher's report. Some will value this more highly than paper qualifications.

Equally, students often take more notice of an employer's report than they do of a teacher's. Don't despair. Employers can in this respect become useful allies to the teacher. Poor reports can be a learning experience provided the criticism is constructive and designed to help the student learn from his/her mistakes.

Employer feedback, then, has a dual function: first to allow the employer to comment on the placement as a whole, and second, to allow the employer to comment on the student in particular. It should be made clear that the *methods* of enabling this feedback to take place are paramount.

Some suggested methods are:

1   Employer's 'open' report
Encourage the employer to discuss the placement with the student on the last afternoon, as a natural follow on to the initial discussion which took place during induction. Again employers will probably need help with this. A review of placement form included in the student's diary would assist both employer and student to focus their discussion (see Appendix 5.3, page 109). This may go alongside the student's self-appraisal form (see Appendix 5.2, page 108). So that the completion of each form evolves from a discussion between employer and student – a discussion which the teacher has facilitated (but not directed).

Employers may also be invited to take part in the debriefing of pupils at school, perhaps sitting in or leading small group sessions in the classroom. Many employers are keen to be involved in this and such enthusiasm is a resource which school should think twice about wasting. However, employers do need help, guidance and support if they are to participate in this kind of exercise.

2   Employer's confidential report

The issue of confidentiality itself
Some teachers value and appreciate a confidential report from the employer, which they can then feed back to the student at their own discretion. Teachers need to be aware of issues of confidentiality here.

Many employers are highly sensitive about these reports – and rightly. If they are led to understand that information is confidential then it should remain so. If there are circumstances where a student or parent will be shown the employer's report or told of its contents, then an employer has a right to know this. Parents may demand to see the report and schools need a clear policy on this. An employer can be placed in a difficult situation if they have an angry parent on the phone to them. Schools may then have to face not only angry parents but also an aggrieved employer. A suitably worded caveat at the bottom of the form is advisable for any so-called 'confidential' report.

The value and use of confidential reports
We think it is sound at this point to reflect for a few moments on why we actually want a

confidential report. Teachers need to be reasonably circumspect in the weight they attach to such reports. Reports are likely to be subjective, sometimes offered by employers with little experience of young people and little knowledge of assessment methods. Standards will vary from employer to employer. While subjectivity and standardisation are issues for the teacher, employers nevertheless do appreciate feeling that their comments on the students are respected and sought. You may therefore wish to give employers the opportunity to voice grievances or criticisms. However, in general our view is that the value of an employer's report lies in its being seen as part of the learning process and that therefore it should be openly discussed with the student.

Reports to the school/college will therefore serve the functions of allowing the employer to make comments to the school on the general success or otherwise of the placement, and on the suitability of the pupil placed with them. This can assist the teacher in the matching of pupil to placement in future, and improve the quality of experience offered to other pupils using that employer.

As with all forms of paperwork the problem is often getting the employer to complete the form at all! We believe that employers will be more likely to take the trouble to complete it if they understand its purpose and, most important, its value *to them*. The employer's confidential report form (Appendix 5.6, page 113) includes a brief statement to this effect.

3 Employer's own review of placement

So far, we have focused on the employer's feedback to or about the student. We now look at the student's feedback to the employer.

One of the most common employer grievances is that after the student leaves them at the end of the placement they hear no further about her/him, or from the school/college, until the next time a placement is wanted. A recent survey in the West Country showed that this was one of the things employers most resented. It made them feel used. They very often would like to know how the students are getting on – how they did in their exams, what they are up to now, did they stay on at school, what career they plan to follow. In other words they appreciate students or the school/college keeping in touch. The standard 'thank you' letter does not really meet this need.

They also appreciate some feedback about the general value and appropriateness of the placement. Did the student think it worthwhile? Did the teacher think it worthwhile? In what ways might it have been improved? Was the work given appropriate? It seems a reckless waste of the employer as a resource not to respond to these legitimate requests for feedback.

Teachers visiting students on placement or teachers contacting the employer in the following season may be able to report back on last year's alumni.

If employers do have grievances – either about the student or the general management of the placement by the school/college – then they should be given an opportunity to voice these concerns and to feel that their concerns are being taken into account.

Employers may also be invited to visit the school – perhaps to have a look round, see samples of students' work, copies of diaries and assignments completed around work experience, and have an opportunity to talk to students again, as well as teaching staff and other employers. A buffet lunch or evening, or open afternoon can serve all these functions, as well as being good PR for the school/college. Many employers will find it difficult to get away during a working day, so timing is important. However, an invitation is always appreciated – it's really the thought that counts.

Quality work experience is provided by employers who are committed, reliable, and experienced in this field. This experience enables them to acquire expertise in managing students, in having realistic and informed expectations of them, and in organising their workplace and the student's work schedule in order to give the student a more worthwhile placement.

Finally, don't just rely on students to send 'thank you' letters. It goes without saying that you should also produce your own. No employer is going to be too impressed to receive fulsome thanks from a student, but nothing from the teacher. Naturally you can't write individually to each employer. This may be a chore, especially if you are writing several times to the same firm, possibly at different times of the year, but if they are giving you all those placements, they do merit some acknowledgement! Remember, letters may well go further than the personnel manager who is your contact. They will probably be circulated to all the departments involved. Clearly a standard letter is called for, but this need be neither stereotyped nor long-winded. A simple 'thank you' card may be mailed out and any comments added in a brief PS. The example given in Appendix 5.7 (page 115) can be reproduced on two sides of a card and sent as a postcard. If you want to include any additions to the note there is room to do so. Christmas cards can also be a method of thanking employers.

As you can see, we place great emphasis on the debriefing of employers as well as students, but the bottom line may be this: a committed and reliable employer – one who comes back year after year to offer placements – apart from offering better placements, helps preserve the sanity of the teacher, and reduces his/her workload. The teacher cannot after all go on for ever replacing 'lost' placements – there is not an inexhaustible supply of willing employers. So it is far better to hang on to, and work with (or 'on') the ones you have.

DEBRIEFING OTHER TEACHING STAFF

As with the employer, the debriefing of staff serves a number of objectives:

1   Use of colleagues as a resource in debriefing students
We have already alluded in the sections above to the involvement of other staff in the debriefing process – their participation in group work, and follow-up activities in the classroom.
2   Improving the commitment and understanding of staff in regard to work experience
The above activities also help to increase other staff's understanding of work experience, and its value. The attitude of other staff in the school/college is important in influencing the attitudes of young people towards work experience. More than many other forms of learning, the value of work experience rests heavily on the student's own commitment to it. If the student expects work experience to be a waste of time or exploitative then it will be just that. This is its strength as well as its weakness: it relies heavily on students' own initiative and interest in order to have value. Therefore it is important that other staff are positive in their perception of work experience and can convey this to their pupils.

Having involved your colleagues at all other stages, let them see the fruits of their labours.
3   Giving staff the opportunity to voice their own views and have them taken on board by the coordinator
Staff also need the opportunity to feed back their impressions of the placements they have visited and to pool the feedback they have received from individual students.

An end-of-placement course team meeting or staff meeting to review the work experience is important. It is often at this stage that colleagues display their lack of awareness of the difficulties of finding placements, and of the constraints within which employers are operating. They are often unreasonable in their expectations of employers, failing to understand that work experience is not *intended* to be a teaching or training environment. It is important therefore to focus on what *they* can do to work with employers to improve the quality of the placements you have. Their help can also be sought in finding new placements for next year's students where needed.

APPENDIX 5.1 Employer's open report

WORK EXPERIENCE
EMPLOYER'S OPEN REPORT

Notes
The cooperation of employers in completing this form is very much appreciated.

Your comments can help the student learn from the placement – from mistakes as well as from successes.

The form may be completed by the person who has worked most closely with the student, or whoever the employer feels is best able to complete it. This need not necessarily be someone very senior in the organisation.

Ideally, wherever possible, it should be completed in discussion with the student, so that the person completing it can give reasons for her/his comments as s/he goes along.

Ideally it should be completed on the last day, or near the end of the placement.

Questionnaire

Name of student ....

Name of employer/organisation ....

In what ways, if any, do you feel the student has benefited from the placement?

- Self confidence?
- Maturity?
- Ability to work with others?
- Learning the skills of the job?
- Any other?

In what ways, if any, has the student *not* taken advantage of the learning opportunities available? Please describe.
In what ways, if any, were you particularly pleased with the student? Please describe.
What activities did the student do especially well?
Is there anything you can think of which the student might have done *before* the placement to prepare her/himself better?
What advice would you give the student in applying for a permanent job, training or college place?
In what ways do you feel the student could improve?
Would you be willing to give the student a reference for a job, college or training place?
What could the student do to improve his/her employability?
Any other comment?

Signed .... Date ....

Position in company ....

APPENDIX 5.2   Student's self-appraisal form

WORK EXPERIENCE
STUDENT'S SELF-APPRAISAL
HOW WELL DID I DO?

Punctuality/attendance
How often was I late?

How many days was I absent?

What are the procedures for reporting sickness/lateness?

Did I follow them? If not, why not?

Performance
What activities did I do best?

What activities did I do least well?

Relationships
How did I get on with the other staff?

Is there anything I might have done to make things better?

Dealing with Problems
– Did I have any difficulties connected with the placement? (eg to do with the boss, other workers, the workplace/general environment, the work given, travelling, or lunch breaks, financial problems, etc?) If so, how did I deal with them? Was I successful in dealing with them? If not, why not?

Signed .... Date ....

APPENDIX 5.3 Review of placement form

STUDENT'S REVIEW OF PLACEMENT

In what ways did you find work experience helpful to you as a person? Please tick those below which apply to you and give reasons wherever you can.

- Gained self-confidence.
- Gained maturity.
- Gained a better understanding of what is expected at work.
- Got a more realistic impression of working life.
- Learned what it is like to work longer hours.
- Helped me to make a career choice.
- Made me more independent by being away from school friends.
- Made me stand on my own feet by being in a new environment.
- Made me better able to mix with people by working alongside people of a different age group.
- Learned more about a particular job.
- Learned some useful job skills.
- Learned a lot by talking to friends at school about the placement.
- Learned by listening to others describe their placement and how they got on.
- Any other ways.

In what ways was it BETTER than you expected?

In what ways was it WORSE?

In what ways was it DIFFERENT from what you expected?

What was the most DIFFICULT thing about work experience?

What was the most ENJOYABLE thing?

If another pupil or student were going to do work experience at that workplace, what advice would you give them?

In what ways, if any, do you think the placement should be changed to make it better for a future student?

What advice would you give any student going on work experience for the first time?

Looking back on the placement, is there anything you would do differently, if you could start again?

On the whole, do you think work experience was worthwhile for YOU personally?

Signed .... Date ....

APPENDIX 5.4   Student's sample 'thank you' letter (1)

31, Osterley Terrace,
London SW34

17/6/91

Mrs Mary Stewart,
District Physiotherapist,
Central London Regional Health Authority,
Central London Hospital,
Physiotherapy Dept.,
London W1 3DZ

Dear Mrs Stewart,

re Work Experience Placement – 3–14 June 1991

First may I thank you for giving me the opportunity recently of doing two weeks' work experience in your department. I was made to feel very welcome and could see that, although you were busy, you spent a lot of time explaining things to me. I appreciated this very much.

What I found particularly useful was watching some of the sessions and listening to the staff talk to the patients and encouraging the patients to keep trying. It made me realise that being a physiotherapist is not just a practical or scientific job but also involves skill in dealing with people.

However, just watching can get a bit boring after a while and I enjoyed doing some of the administration too. This helped me to see everything involved in running the department – working out staffing rotas, and making appointments for out-patients. It made me realise why it's so important to be on time for work and the responsibility you have to your colleagues and the patients.

I am planning to stay on at school as you know, to take my 'A' levels. Now I know how important they are for jobs I will work very hard!

I am hoping to take biology, chemistry and one more subject, but I will have to see first how I get on this year. I will write to you again and tell you what I end up doing. I am still hoping to become a doctor and if I succeed I am sure that the experience I have had in your department will always be useful. There are other jobs in the health field I am now also thinking about – now I have seen how many different professions there are.

Please pass on my best wishes to all the staff and thank them for their help.

We are having an open day at our school soon for employers who have had work experience students, when you will be able to have a look round our school and see some of our work. I do hope you are able to accept our invitation to come. Details will follow.

Yours sincerely,

Jackie Gillet.
Student,
St Elmore's College.

APPENDIX 5.5   Student's sample 'thank you' letter (2)

St Mavis School,
Wigmore St,
Newtown

1/3/91

Supreme Garage,
Back St,
Newtown.

Dear Steve,

re work experience – 4–8 March 1991

I am writing to thank you for letting me do work experience in your garage.

I enjoyed working on the cars and find this very useful. It gave me a chance to really see all the things which have to be done in a garage.

I am sorry I was late on Tuesday but I overslept as I was up late the night before, then I missed the bus. I am not used to having to start so early. Now at least I have learnt what it's like! I did not realise it would make such a difference to you if I didn't turn up, and I couldn't find a phone which was working.

Please say hello to the others in the garage and I hope I have not been in their way.

I hope you will come to our school's open day next month. The details will follow.

I hope you will consider taking pupils from this school for work experience in the future as there are lots of pupils who want to do motor mechanics, and it is very useful to find out what the work is really like.

Yours sincerely,

Dexter Watkinson
Pupil at St Mavis School

APPENDIX 5.6 Employer's confidential report form

WORK EXPERIENCE
EMPLOYER'S CONFIDENTIAL REPORT FORM

Guidance notes for employers

We are grateful to you for having accepted (one of) our students into your workplace for work experience. As a school/college we place a high value on our relationships with the local community and the support we receive from employers. We are therefore pleased to have your comments and criticisms, in order to:

- Help us to help the student.
- Help us better prepare the students for their work experience.
- Help us make a better match of student to your placement, ie help us (in future) to identify students who are best able to benefit from the experience you are offering.
- Help us to ensure that the support we give you in the supervision of our students is appropriate to your needs.
- Help us improve our methods of setting up and 'managing' work experience.

The information or comments given by you in Part One of this form are not normally shown routinely to pupils. However, this report form may be shown to students' parents or parents/guardians if a specific request is made.

Teachers *may* also feed back to students, individually or as a group, the *general nature* of your comments and suggestions, as part of the overall review of the placement.

The student's work experience diary includes an open employer report form where you have the opportunity to comment more fully on the student's performance.

Would you be kind enough to take the time to complete the questionnaire as fully as possible and return it to:

Questionnaire

Name of student ....

Name and address of employer ....

....

Part One

Would you comment on the student's general suitability for the placement:

1 Interest in the work?
2 Punctuality/attendance?
3 Aptitude?
4 Relationships with others?

113

5 Temperament/personality?
6 Strengths/weaknesses
7 Any other comments?

Part Two

Do you have any suggestions for improvement in the following areas?

1 Methods used by school/college in approaching employers, eg length of notice, initial visits by staff, forms and letters used.

2 Initial introduction of student to employer – student arranging own 'interview', letter of introduction, general preparedness of student, etc.

3 General preparation of student.

4 Information given about school, college, course of study, etc.

5 Support offered during the placement, eg staff visits, help if problems arose.

6 Dates/length of placement.

7 Employer's report forms.

8 Do you have any suggestions for improvement in any other areas?

9 Which, if any, of the above areas do you think should be the school's priority for improvement?

Thank you for your time and interest.

Signed .... Date ....

Position in company ....

APPENDIX 5.7   An official 'thank you' card

THANKS

FROM

ST OSWALD'S COLLEGE

Thank you for taking student

on work experience. The student enjoyed the placement and found it very valuable.

We are all grateful to you and your colleagues for your help.

Signed .... (Tutor)

APPENDIX 5.8 Student's work experience certificate

STUDENT'S
WORK EXPERIENCE CERTIFICATE

This is to certify that

Student's name _____

School _____

HAS SUCCESSFULLY COMPLETED
TWO WEEKS' WORK EXPERIENCE

AT

Company _____

Address _____

Signed _____

Position _____

Date _____

6
Special issues

So far, we have looked at fairly straightforward issues as they affect the average student going on work experience. But your situation and your students will rarely conform to this 'norm'. What if you are dealing with groups or individuals who have special needs? Suppose you or the students have to contend with racism or sexism? How do you cope or react in these circumstances, which are by no means unusual?

In this chapter, we shall be looking at these special issues which mainly centre around equal opportunities of one kind or another. We shall be building on the good practice described in the rest of the book, as dealing with these issues relies even more heavily on a coordinated, well-prepared and well-documented approach.

SPECIAL NEEDS STUDENTS

We are using this term as a catch-all heading, but it does refer to three discrete groups of students:

1 Those with special educational needs.
2 Those with special physical needs.
3 Bilingual students.

Even though the above takes in a very broad range of students, when it comes to work experience, they have several features in common. So before considering each group separately, let us look at these common issues, the main one of which is:

Employer attitude

Two points immediately arise here:

1 However well disposed they are, many employers shy away from taking special needs students on placement. This attitude is often based on the premise that they will involve more

time and effort than other students. The thinking goes along these lines – taking on a so-called average student can be time-consuming and cause a fair amount of disruption in the workplace, so to have one who has 'special needs' is just *asking* for trouble.

From the employer's point of view, this may indeed be a reasonable initial standpoint. Before you rush to disagree, remember that you, as a teacher, have training and experience with special needs students. An employer is often operating from a totally different base.

2   The employer may only have a vague perception of what 'special needs' are. As in any other profession, educationalists are inclined to use jargon and to assume that 'outsiders' understand it. Many employers faced with the term 'special needs' visualise a student in a wheelchair. Others may nod sagely when you introduce the phrase, without really understanding what it means. As for 'bilingual', to a lot of people, this conjures up visions of someone who speaks fluent French and German, rather than someone whose first language isn't English.

Your approach

This is where you come in! There is nothing in the viewpoints above that can't be remedied by a positive attitude and good communications.

If you are doing an initial mailshot on behalf of a particular group of students, it is probably best to spell things out in a matter-of-fact way in an accompanying leaflet, along the lines of:

> This group of St Oswald's students has various special needs such as learning difficulties, Downs Syndrome and behavioural problems. The course aims to teach them the skills which they will need as young adults in a modern world. Subjects covered include communications, numeracy, cooking, health education, and sport.
>
> All the students involved in the work experience have been specially selected to go on placement. Once their course is finished, they will be helped to live independently and to find full-time work. In the past, students from this course have gone on to obtain jobs as machinists, catering workers, messengers, office post-room assistants and warehouse staff.

Something like this meets key issues head on, while being concise, jargon-free and very much orientated towards what the students *can* do. What employers fear most in these situations is the *unknown*. If you can show them that taking on a special needs student isn't as alarming as it first appears, then they are going to be much more receptive to the whole idea. Most employers who become involved in work experience genuinely want to help – but they can't if they don't have the necessary information.

If you are meeting the employer on a face-to-face basis (and at some point a pre-placement visit is most definitely called for), aim to get your verbal message across in the same succinct fashion. This is also true if you are only looking for a one-off special needs placement.

Describe the student to the employer in terms of how their needs might affect that employer, eg the kind of extra support they might need while at work. You may say, for example, 'she is as mature as any other young person her age and able to get along with people. Her reading and writing ability is *not* what you would expect from a sixteen-year-old', or 'he is hardworking, but has had a very sheltered life and will need a little more patience than others of his age'.

It may seem to you while visiting a workplace or looking through a placement description form that it would be ideal for that particular student. Take the bull by the horns! Write, phone or simply say, 'I think that this would suit one of our students, who has impaired hearing. Do you think that you could help?'

LAYING THE GROUNDWORK

Naturally the employer will want more information – for instance, does Lee lipread? Will any special devices, such as amplification to the phones be needed? If so, where will they come from and who is paying for them?

Do your homework on these matters *before* you approach the employer. Don't lose out on a good placement by not having the facts at your fingertips. You do not want the employer to back out because it all sounds rather vague or disorganised.

However, be realistic. It is no good sending a special needs student to a placement where he or she is not going to be able to contribute as fully as possible. This will only make the student unhappy and disillusioned, as it will the staff in the workplace, who are giving up their time and resources.

Assess what the student can reasonably do – and do try to look at it from the employer's point of view. You may well assure the personnel manager that Maria is one of your best students in English, but this doesn't necessarily mean that she can do the jobs which the firm had in mind. She may be coming on apace in the English classes, but how will she cope with filing and addressing envelopes?

COMMUNICATION DIFFICULTIES

Students with any form of communication difficulties are in a particularly awkward position. They may not be able to cope with seemingly straightforward tasks such as answering the phone or relaying messages. They could be unable to establish relationships with their colleagues and with members of the public. This can result in great unhappiness and frustration for the student, particularly if workmates find it too embarrassing or time-consuming to persist in establishing effective communications.

It can also result in general chaos at the workplace. We know of incidents where firms couldn't cope with the demands of students who were bilingual. These firms had taken on the students in all good faith, but had not been sufficiently well briefed. When the difficulties started affecting both staff and work output, they felt that they had to call a halt. This soured relations between the parties involved. One further effect was on the students themselves who had passed a most bewildering time. The tutors who placed them had obviously thought that they were acting for the best, without considering the full implications of the situation.

Motto: when in doubt, stop and take stock. Try to envisage yourself in that particular situation. How would you feel if you were left in, say, Yugoslavia for a fortnight, with only a limited knowledge of Serbo-Croat and no one around you who could speak English? Oh, and you would be expected to do a full day's work too! We would say that it is downright cruel to expose students to such difficulties in the name of work experience.

This *is* work experience not an extended English class. The students go on placement primarily to acquire knowledge of the world of work and to build up their social skills – including their self-confidence. Anything which detracts from these objectives may not be in the students' best interests. To combine work experience with mastering new communication skills may not be fair on certain special needs groups. In that case they may need more sheltered placements where English language skills are not paramount. In some instances, work-shadowing/work simulation could be more appropriate.

FINDING THE PLACEMENTS

Providing the above guidelines are followed, there is no reason why finding placements for students with any form of special needs should differ from the process described in Chapter 2. The sections on your placement description form (Appendix 3.4, Supplementary details section) covering languages spoken and facilities for physically handicapped students come into their own here.

If difficulties arise or placements are in short supply, consider these placement ideas:

All special needs students

- Local government.
- Civil Service.

Both of these groups are usually well aware of special needs issues and often have specialist facilities to deal with them.

Special educational/physical needs

- Special Needs Careers Officers/Disablement Resettlement Officers in Job Centres.
- Charities and voluntary organisations, eg MIND, Royal National Institute for the Deaf.

Bilingual students

- Community bodies, eg ethnic theatre companies, local associations for particular cultural groups.
- Black/Asian Chambers of Commerce.
- LEA language coordinators, specialist youth workers.
- Religious institutions/organisations.
- Refugee organisations.

These groups may not necessarily be able to provide placements but will usually have specialist personnel who can advise on sympathetic employers and practical issues which may affect the student when on work experience.

STUDENT AND EMPLOYER PREPARATION

The basic tenet behind the preceding pages is: 'Make sure that both students and employers have an accurate idea of what is expected of them.' Visits to the workplace by you and the students are vital. No matter how carefully you have checked out the placement and discussed the finer points, the student is the best judge of how suitable it is. You may, for example, have assiduously vetted a firm to make sure that it has the right facilities for a wheelchair-bound student. But it is the student who will know that there is no room to manoeuvre a wheelchair in the allocated department or that the toilets are unsuitable.

For many students, it may be best to 'ease' them into the work experience by attending for one or two days a week before the main placement starts. Certainly some students will need 'travel training'. For those with physical handicaps, such as visual impairments, this may involve learning a new route and/or the best method of transport to take. For students with learning difficulties, it could involve researching and using public transport routes – possibly for the first time. There is no way that this process can be anything other than time-consuming. It may even involve the tutor in trailing the student to the workplace. In every other respect, preparation should follow the pattern outlined in Chapter 3 – all of these key elements are as important for special needs students as for anyone else. The materials we have suggested in Chapter 3 can be simplified, if necessary, and adapted for various groups of special needs students. Some organisations, such as Youth Education Service Publications (Hebron House, Bedminster, Bristol BS3 3BD) produce work experience materials specifically aimed at these groups. Of course, your involvement will not end at the preparation stage, because these students may need extra support while they are actually on placement – even to the extent of daily phone calls or visits. Don't go overboard, though. Give both student and employer room to breathe. If it is viable, suggest that the student phones *you* at a set time to report on progress.

Special needs is one matter, racism and sexism are other issues which could affect any of your students on work experience. What practical steps can you take to prevent this happening and what should you do, if, despite your best efforts, a sexist or racist incident occurs?

PRE-PLACEMENT TACTICS: EMPLOYERS

It starts (like everything else, it seems) when you first approach an employer. Your initial mailshot and any explanatory literature should bear the magic phrase 'St Oswald's is an equal opportunities college'. You can extend this if you wish by listing those to whom the equal opportunities apply, eg 'regardless of race, colour, disability', but it is the initial phrase which is important. It clearly delineates your position from the beginning and may warn off employers who are not interested in providing equal opportunities.

You may, when you go to visit, ask an employer if the company has an equal opportunities code of practice and possibly ask to see or keep a copy. Be careful how you handle this as some perfectly bona fide organisations and many respectable smaller firms won't have drawn up such a code. And any employer may become indignant if the request is clumsily phrased or totally inappropriate to the conversation. However, such documents are very useful, partly because they often differ very widely from firm to firm. They show that the employer has given equal opportunities some thought, but in themselves they are no guarantee that a sexist or racist incident won't occur – just as lack of a policy isn't necessarily a harbinger of doom.

The real test of a company's equal opportunities viewpoint comes when you give the employer details of a student's name or sex. If this information causes a reaction such as 'I don't want any coloureds', at least you know where you stand, however reprehensible such a statement may be. But most discrimination is more subtle than this and examples of phrases that might start warning bells ringing are given in Table 6.1. As with our case studies, all are taken from 'real life' and show that employers are likely to be far more overt about sex discrimination than its racial equivalent. Sex stereotyping is often still seen to be acceptable by some employers.

Table 6.1 *Phrases to note*

'That's an unusual name – where does he come from?'

'We don't have any facilities for young ladies.'

'Is she a British citizen?'

'It's not really a boy's job.'

'We'd like someone strong – there's a lot of heavy lifting.'

'Does he speak English?'

'It's a mainly female workforce.'

'I don't think she'd fit in here.'

Of course, even if an employer does voice any of these ideas, they may not be intending to discriminate – merely voicing concerns which it is your role to allay. Your immediate response might be to challenge their statement quite forcefully, but at this stage, tread warily. Many employers may not even realise that their remarks are discriminatory or offensive: they can often be persuaded to your way of thinking quite simply. Only if they persist in their original line do you have to point out that what they are saying is illegal and that your school or college will not be a party to it. *This is a legal obligation on your part too. If you condone or comply with their preferences, your institution could be laying itself open to court action.*

If you are not getting any satisfaction from the employer, the bald statement of fact about the illegality of discrimination is all that you need make. Don't be drawn into an argument, become angry or upset. A far better alternative is to write to the employer or to the relevant head office expressing your feelings in writing (in which case keep a copy for yourself). But whatever else you document, make sure that the incident is clearly noted on all relevant files, eg computer database, placement details forms and cards. If there is a work experience co-ordinator contact him/her in writing too.

So far everything has been pretty clear-cut: either employers are being discriminatory or they are not. But not all incidents can be categorised so neatly. Here is a situation which is ambivalent:

> You have sent Lauren, an Afro-Caribbean student, for a pre-placement interview with a ladies' fashion chain store. When you phone, the manager explains that she didn't come over well and that the firm would rather not take her on work experience. Lauren is disappointed but does confirm that she performed badly at interview. The manager's rejection could be for a genuine reason or it could be racist. What, if anything, do you do?

In this case, we would suggest you give the employer the benefit of the doubt – having first checked with the files and the work experience coordinator that nothing similar has happened at this store or one of their other branches. Again, be sure to annotate your records for future reference.

PRE-PLACEMENT TACTICS: STAFF AND STUDENTS

It is important that both staff and students are aware that racist and sexist incidents may happen on placement. It is equally important that they feel prepared to cope with them and that they know that they have the backing of those in authority. To deal with the last point first, your school/college may itself have an equal opportunities policy and this should be integrated into preparations for work experience, both verbally and in written form. If there is no such policy why not draft one? – possibly based around the work experience and hopefully with some input from the staff and students involved. See Appendices 6.1 and 6.2 for examples (pages 126 and 127).

Students should know that any problems of racism/sexism will be treated seriously by the staff monitoring the placement and staff need to be equipped to handle such problems. So far, we have talked about tutors interceding on the student's behalf, but this may not always be the case. Some students will want to deal with the problem by themselves, but they will need advice and backing. Others may want no action – or only limited action – to be taken. For them, it might be sufficient that the problem has been discussed and *acknowledged*. Problems are more likely to arise if incidents are played down or ignored by monitoring staff or if the student does not feel that he/she will get a sympathetic hearing. No one wants a genuine grievance dismissed as over-reacting.

Having said this, there may be genuine instances when racist or sexist behaviour is unintentional and founded on ignorance rather than malice. The concept of equal opportunities and an understanding of other cultures was in many ways pioneered by the education sector and we are often way ahead of industry and commerce in this respect. The following examples illustrate the point:

> A large hotel group was disconcerted when a female Bengali student turned up for work experience wearing trousers. This was against company policy and the young woman was reassigned to behind-the-scenes clerical duties rather than the front-of-house role originally planned. When the monitoring tutor challenged this action, it transpired that none of the

hotel management had realised that these clothes were being worn for religious/cultural reasons. They had thought that the girl was ignoring the dress code which they had laid down for all staff. Once the situation was explained, they reinstated the student in her placement on the reception desk *and* reviewed their general policy towards the wearing of trousers by female employees.

Two Nigerian students were sent on work experience to the same firm. Assigned to separate duties, they met up at breaks and lunch times, when they would chat in their own language. Co-workers complained – they construed this as unfriendly and were unhappy that the students might be making derogatory remarks about the firm and its staff. The students, who had intended no offence, thought that they were the victims of discrimination. The situation was resolved by the work experience coordinator, who visited the organisation, discussed it with all concerned and was able to restore good relations between the parties.

Each of the above situations was the result of lack of understanding and poor communications. In both cases the difficulties were sorted out speedily and amicably and important lessons were learned by all involved.

Pause for a moment and consider the consequences if the incidents had been ignored or played down. What if the work experience coordinator had reacted angrily rather than listening to both parties, or if she had not visited in person? In these instances there is no substitute for face-to-face dialogue.

Of course, not all incidents are so easily resolved. And many are genuinely blatant discrimination, eg racist abuse or sexual harassment, which can be very upsetting indeed.

What should you do in these circumstances? Well, no one piece of advice can cover every contingency, but a good starting-point is the code of practice above. The essential step is to get clear *written* details as soon as possible. Keep your own notes too and update any documents, such as files.

For serious and possibly contentious issues, you will want to inform line managers and perhaps HODs, headteachers, principals, etc. They have a right to know what has happened and an obligation to advise and support. If a complaint is to be made, you should be able to expect backing at senior level and this will add weight to your case. Discuss issues and courses of action with senior colleagues and keep notes of outcomes. As we have said, there is no substitute for personal visits and there is no harm in suggesting that a colleague or line manager accompanies you if the situation seems to warrant it.

Students themselves may not want to take any further action, to save themselves further distress. Sensitivity to their wishes and views is paramount. Simply being withdrawn from the placement or for the offending behaviour to stop may be all they want. But this does not mean that the issues could not be drawn to the attention of the employer, provided that this is done with due regard to the student's views and feelings.

Where applicable, racist and sexist behaviour should also be raised with the senior management or even the head office at the placement. There is no way that they can rectify grievances or prevent them recurring if they don't know about them. And even if they trivialise or ignore your complaints, at least they know exactly what your stance is on such issues. Who knows, they may even learn something from it.

The alternative is never to use those placements again, but to give no explanation for this course of action. In which case, nothing would have come out of the difficulties suffered by the students, the problems would have been swept under the carpet, and the offenders would have got off scot-free.

Of course, the majority of students, whatever their background, don't experience massive difficulties on work experience. None the less, it is important to bear in mind what could happen and to be alert for any warning signs of minor problems escalating into major incidents. This isn't alarmist – it's common sense. When it comes to the issues raised in this chapter, you won't go far wrong if you make 'Be Prepared' your motto.

APPENDIX 6.1   Equal opportunities policy – gender

- Do not make assumptions about the expectation of students to enter 'traditional' sex-stereotyped jobs on work experience.
- Make students aware of the possibility of entering 'non-traditional' areas of work while on placement.
- Enhance students' awareness of the value of sampling non-traditional jobs through work experience.
- Use preparation for work experience as a chance to discuss equal opportunities at work, and work-related problems which may be faced by women, eg child care, sexual harassment.
- Investigate all suspicions or allegations of discrimination on work experience.
- Ensure that students are aware of the school or college's equal opportunities policy and that they know whom to contact if problems arise.
- Make employers aware of this policy at an early stage in negotiations.
- Do not pre-select students (or bow to pressure from employers to pre-select) on the grounds of gender.
- Do not make assumptions about employers' expectations regarding the gender of students.
- Discuss with/challenge employers' claims to exemption under the Sex Discrimination Act and their stated assumptions/prejudices regarding students' gender.
- Do not use placements where employers have indicated an intention to discriminate, directly or indirectly, either when they select students or in the type of work they give students.
- Monitor all placements to ensure this policy is being observed.
- Keep records of all instances of discrimination, suspected discrimination, or other sexist practices, so that a picture of employers can be built up on file and remedial action taken where appropriate.
- Where there is clear evidence of discrimination, and attempts to resolve the issue have failed, refer the matter to the headteacher or principal, who should write to the employer giving reasons why the placement will not be used.

APPENDIX 6.2 Equal opportunities policy – race, religion, ethnicity

- Ensure that all parties are aware of the school/college's policy on equal opportunities at an early stage and in a manner which is clear and assertive but which does not threaten or accuse.
- Discuss with students issues to do with equal opportunities at work as part of their preparation for work experience. Help them to know how to deal with racism in a confident and mature way.
- Ensure that students know with whom they can discuss any concerns they have about issues of equal opportunities, and encourage them to do so.
- Try to ensure that this person is someone in whom the students have confidence and trust.
- Try to ensure that students feel their concerns will be treated seriously and sympathetically and that their wishes will be paramount.
- Do not use placements where you have reason to believe there will be discrimination, or racism.
- Do not collude with employers in any way in discriminatory practices, eg by agreeing to send only white pupils to a particular placement (even where the pupil you have in mind for the placement is white).
- Where discrimination or racist attitudes are suspected, follow the agreed guidelines for dealing with it.
- Do not inflame a situation by accusing employers of racist attitudes, or implying the same, unless the evidence is clear and you have given them the opportunity of rectifying mistakes.
- Wherever possible or necessary, try to educate employers about cultural or religious differences which may affect working practices and seek their sympathetic support. Encourage them to accommodate such differences, eg on questions of dress, religious festivals, or prayer times.
- Take account of religious practices which may affect the placement when planning work experience, eg religious holidays.
- Take account of students' domestic circumstances and responsibilities when planning work experience, eg acting as translators for parents, housework, child care, family business or other domestic responsibilities, willingness to travel out of immediate area.
- Log all instances of discrimination, suspected discrimination, or racist attitudes or practices. Keep notes of conversations, where appropriate.
- Refer clear cases of discrimination to the headteacher or principal so that employers can be informed of a decision not to use their placement and reasons given.

Conclusion

If one had to summarise in one word the key to successful work experience it would be COMMUNICATION.

Use *every* kind of communication:

- talk to people personally
- hold meetings
- encourage telephone contact
- give written guidance wherever possible
- confirm everything in writing
- encourage discussion within your own institution
- encourage communication and discussion within the organisations of your placement providers.

Communicate with *all the parties* involved:

- pupils and students
- employers and others in the workplace
- parents
- teaching colleagues – form/course tutors
- headteachers, heads of year, heads of faculty.

Encourage full communication/discussion *between* the parties about practical arrangements, expectations, concerns, anxieties, problems:

- employer with student, and vice versa
- parent with school/employer and vice versa
- teacher visiting placement with employer/other staff/student, and vice versa.

Communicate at all *stages* of the process:

- communicate your aims and objectives

- spell out the practical arrangements in writing, confirm on the telephone, where needed, encourage all parties to talk to you if there is anything which is not clear
- encourage communication *during* the placement
- encourage pupils to discuss placement arrangements or any problems with employer/school, and vice versa
- encourage employer to contact school to discuss any worries
- communicate *at end of* the placement
- encourage employer to feed back to student, and vice versa
- encourage school to feed back to employer, and vice versa
- encourage students to feed back to each other, and so on
- provide written materials to support and encourage communication.

Most importantly of all, communicate enthusiasm. More so than any other form of learning, work experience, by its very nature, will depend on the attitude and enthusiasm of the participants. The learning opportunities of a work placement are many – but rest upon the student being pro-active in taking them.

The introduction of work experience into the curriculum is probably one of the most profound and far-reaching changes which the school curriculum has undergone in the last 20 years. Those of us who have been involved in education–employer links have come to realise the energy and the wealth of goodwill which exists among employers towards education. Employers represent a huge resource at the door of education – one whose potential is still far from being fully realised, and it is the education side of this equation which is in the driving seat.

Those employers motivated by short-term goals, expecting to get more than they give, can be weeded out or indeed will weed themselves out fairly quickly. For most employers, supporting education is – as a representative of the Banking Information Service has put it – a question of 'enlightened long-term self-interest'.

We should furthermore remind ourselves that 'employers' span the whole spectrum of the community at large – public sector organisations like the National Health Service, voluntary bodies, charities, professional bodies, local authorities' departments, community and welfare groups, theatres and youth centres, day nurseries, and a whole host of other types of organisations – as well as the more commercially operated organisations. The failure to harness this immense and valuable resource would be profligate waste and a disservice to our young people.

We hope, therefore, that above all this book will strengthen your conviction of the value and potential of work experience and give you that most valuable resource of all – enthusiasm.

Appendix I
Case studies

The following case studies describe the kinds of problems which can develop when running work experience.

All the cases used in this book are taken from real life (but names and any other identifying features have been changed). They are not unusual or exceptional.

The case studies below are selected to focus on and illustrate some key points:

1   The need to be clear about objectives.
2   The importance of common goals and shared perceptions among the parties concerned.
3   The importance of effective communication of goals.
4   The importance of taking account of and being sensitive to issues of equal opportunities.
5   The need to support the employer and the student during the placement.
6   The importance of student preparation, particularly with respect to 'coping' strategies and dealing with problems.

Consider each of the case studies in relation to the following questions and points:

- In what ways was the placement successful?
- Identify positive aspects of each case study and consider what contributed to this success.
- What objectives are appropriate for this particular placement?
- What relative emphasis should you place on your objectives?
- What steps might have been taken to communicate these more effectively to the parties concerned?
- In what ways have issues of equal opportunities been a factor in the success of the placement?
- What might you do now to achieve success?

Case Study 1
You have sweated blood to find a placement for Jo, who is doing GCSE resits in the sixth form. Work experience is optional. Jo has requested a placement working with a plumber. Your

school has a well-developed work experience preparation programme and you are satisfied that Jo has realistic expectations and understands the broader objectives of the placement. As the student is so highly motivated and has realistic aspirations, you feel it is worth the effort of finding just the right placement. A parental consent form went out earlier in the year, and this was returned duly signed. The day before the placement is due to start, Jo's dad rings you to say that no child of his will be exploited in this way – 'over his dead body'. Nothing you can say will placate the father. Jo is bitterly disappointed but finds it hard to defy the father.

Case Study 2
Shazia is a 15-year-old bilingual pupil receiving extra support with the English language. She is able but lacks confidence. You feel that it is particularly important that she has the opportunity to do work experience. You have worked hard with her, accompanying her on her initial visit to the placement. You are pleased with yourself for having found a caring, supportive employer who understands Shazia's needs. She is both nervous and excited. A letter had been sent earlier in the year to her parents, translated into her mother tongue. The day before the placement is due to start, Shazia tells you she is unable to do the work experience because her father has forbidden her to travel to the town centre alone. There are no suitable placements nearer home.

Case Study 3
Nadia is successfully placed with a large prestigious firm of financial consultants. The premises are very 'up-market' and Nadia has dressed appropriately. She is enjoying the placement and is doing well. Half-way through, Mrs Brown, the Senior Personnel Manager, with whom you originally negotiated the placement, calls to complain. A member of teaching staff had arrived unannounced to see Nadia. This caused some disruption as they work on an appointments system. Furthermore, although the teacher, Mr Jones, spoke briefly to Nadia and to her '1st line supervisor', Liz, he did not speak to Mrs Brown herself, who didn't even find out about the visit until afterwards. Mrs Brown feels that, while she has no complaints about Nadia, she would have liked the opportunity to discuss Nadia's progress with her teacher and in any case thinks he might have had the courtesy to introduce himself. Later you speak to Nadia, who tells you how embarrassed she was by Mr Jones's visit, especially as he arrived wearing jeans. He asked her if everything was all right, and then left. Nadia feels let down. You know that, as there are few teachers able to do visits, simply taking him off the job is not an option. Furthermore, this is a teacher with seniority over you.

Case Study 4
Jennifer is a hard-working, pleasant 5th-year pupil at a comprehensive school in a working-class area. She is thinking of staying on for a CPVE course or perhaps taking further GCSEs. She has ambitions to become a solicitor. Her Careers Officer has advised her of entry qualifications and of the other opportunities available in the legal field requiring fewer qualifications. Jennifer is now also considering these. Placements in the legal field are hard to find in your area and the firms are old-fashioned and rather snobby. Nevertheless you succeed in placing her in a large legal practice. Two days into the placement the Senior Partner, a man nearing retirement, rings you. He tells you that in his opinion Jennifer has poor personal

presentation and communication skills and is unsuited to employment of any kind in this firm. He is sending her back.

Case Study 5

George is a 15-year-old and does not want to do work experience at all unless it is with the specific firm of his choice and in the occupation of his choice. He truanted from most of the work experience preparation sessions. It was not possible to find him the placement of his choice and you feel you have offered a reasonable alternative and explained the objectives carefully. He still refuses the placement. He is a stroppy pupil at the best of times and you are a teacher with a reputation for firm control, a reputation you wish to maintain. Eventually you lose patience and order George to go to the placement. After a week the employer sends George back. Apparently George had made it clear to the employer that he didn't wish to be there. Furthermore, he had been late three times already. Mr Bloggs is angry with the school and with George for wasting his time.

Case Study 6

Fred is a pupil with learning difficulties. He lacks confidence and has never used public transport alone. He will be leaving school soon as he and his parents both need and want him to earn a living. You are pleased to have found a caring placement for him, working in the kitchen of a day centre for the elderly, serving the food and helping the residents eat, where necessary.

You have practised the transport route with him. The superintendent of the home, Maria, understands his needs and the objectives of the placement. However, after a few days Fred turns up back at school distressed because the staff were snappy and irritable with him, complaining that he is slow and in their way.

You ring Maria to discuss the situation. She is quite happy for Fred to come back and says she will talk to the staff. However, she points out that she has 20 very dependent clients in her home, that it is difficult to find good staff and she considers herself lucky to have such a capable and caring workforce. She admits there might have been fault on their part but points out the stresses they are under and feels they have given a good deal of their time and patience to Fred. Who can blame them for resenting having to 'carry' a fellow worker?

Case Study 7

Taleya's placement in a hairdressing salon was fixed up by your local Work Experience Coordinator. On Wednesday afternoon of the first week you see her hanging around the school playground and ask her why she isn't at her placement. She replies that the work is boring, that all she is doing is sweeping up hair and making tea. She doesn't feel she is learning anything. Since Taleya is a bright girl and is usually conscientious and hard-working you feel sympathetic and offer to see if another placement can be found for her.

You ring the Work Experience Coordinator who seems reluctant to help and suggests you ring the employer yourself before she will take any action.

You have no free time on Wednesday so it is Thursday before you get to speak to Mrs Kyriacou, the employer. Mrs Kyriacou tells you that Taleya worked well on Monday and Tuesday morning, but went out at lunchtime and didn't come back. Mrs Kyriacou had been very worried about her and thought she might have had an accident. She had tried to ring the school but found it difficult to get through. The line is constantly busy and when she does get through she keeps being put through to the staffroom and you're not there. She is told to ring back at break, between 10.50 and 10.55 am. (Your breaks are spent walking between sites so there's only five minutes when you're contactable.) She can't keep popping out to make phone calls when she has customers waiting.

She tells you that all trainees start out doing the routine tasks and she had no idea that Taleya was unhappy. Monday is always a quiet day. Tuesday and Thursday evenings are their 'model nights' when staff get to practise techniques on each other and on volunteer 'models'. If she wants she can come to the 'model nights'. This is part of staff's normal working hours but she doesn't mind if Taleya takes time off to compensate.

It is Friday before you get to speak to Taleya again, who is still not really happy about going back. The Work Experience Coordinator tells you it is now too late to find an alternative placement at such short notice when there is only a week left to go anyway.

Case Study 8

Andreas is placed in a firm of lift engineers doing on-site maintenance of lifts. He rings you to complain that he was sent home on his second day because he arrived five minutes late and they had already gone to the site without him.

On the third day a job which was scheduled to take all day was finished by midday and Bill, the engineer he was assigned to, decided to go home early. (Andreas suspects Bill of working 'on the side'.) Bill sent Andreas back to the depot to see the foreman. Andreas spent all day hanging around as all the other engineers were already out on jobs and there wasn't really much for him to do.

On the fourth day he was given a row by Bill for arriving late again and causing him to have to wait. Bill reminded Andreas that he is on bonus and waiting for him is costing him money.

You visit the workplace and discuss the situation with Mike the foreman, with whom you arranged the placement. According to Mike, Andreas was also late on the first day (something Andreas omitted to mention) and that he was told then how important it is to arrive on time. On the second day he was fifteen minutes late – not five minutes.

Mike points out how much trouble he took to fix up the placement and persuade the engineers to have a work experience student with them. Bill had complained that work experience students are more of a hindrance than a help and that Andreas seems half asleep most of the time anyway. He doesn't really want him.

Andreas is still keen to do the placement. He says he can always get a job in a Greek restaurant where most of his family work and he has plenty of contacts who will help him. (He already has a part-time job.) However, he really wants to be an engineer and hopes this placement – if successful – will help him get into a college course.

Case Study 9

Meena is a shy pupil of limited ability but you feel she could probably cope with a placement involving fairly routine clerical tasks. You place her in the office of a large insurance company, with an employer who you feel is prepared to make a real effort for her.

At the end of the first week the employer, Mr Smythe, rings to say he finds Meena very hard work. It is difficult to get anything out of her and he doesn't know how she is feeling or what she is thinking. She makes lots of mistakes with the typing, muddles up the photocopying, and keeps filing things wrongly. He wouldn't mind if only she'd *say* if she can't cope, or *ask* if she doesn't understanding something, rather than just going off and spending half the morning doing it wrongly!

He says he has made a real effort to make her feel welcome, and introduces her to everyone as she goes along. He has moved her round several departments in order to give her variety and to let her meet new people as he thought this would be good for her, but she doesn't seem to be coming out of her shell at all. In fact she seems to be retreating further into it and her mistakes and muddles are getting worse. He's afraid his staff will lose patience.

Some key points raised

Case Study 1

Factors contributing to success:

- Jo's career aspirations taken into account, leading to high motivation.
- Well-developed work experience preparation programme ensures Jo is aware of broader objectives.

Obstacles to success:

- Jo's father inadequately briefed – does not understand broader objectives of placement – does not appreciate broad vocational awareness, and life and social skills as an element of work experience objectives.

Other issues to consider:

- Is Jo's gender significant here?

Remedies:
- Parents' evening specifically on work experience.
- Improved parents' briefing materials.
- Greater parental involvement in placement finding.
- Discussion with students about parental support as part of the preparation programme might have enabled the teacher to anticipate difficulties and deal with them at an earlier stage.

Case Study 2

Factors contributing to success:

- Employer well briefed.
- Pupil carefully prepared – is motivated and supported.
- Letter to parent translated to mother tongue.

Obstacles to success:

- Inadequate briefing of parent – does not understand broad objectives of placement.
- Insufficient account taken of cultural differences.

Remedies:

- As for Case Study 1.

Case Study 3
Factors contributing to success:

- Highly motivated student.
- Concerned and involved employer – wishes to discuss Nadia's progress in a positive way – not simply to voice complaints.

Obstacles to success:

- Inadequately briefed teacher – sees monitoring as a one-off visit rather than an on-going process – lack of awareness of employer needs – does not see supporting employer as one of the objectives of visit.
- Teacher possibly lacks awareness of the objectives of placement.
- Teacher possibly does not really see importance of visit – not taking it seriously enough.

Remedies

- Improved briefing materials for teachers.
- INSET for staff doing monitoring visit.

Case Study 4
Factors contributing to success:

- Advice of Careers Officer sought, leading to student being better informed and realistic about objectives of placement.
- Motivated student.

Obstacles to success:

- Inadequate briefing of employer – seems to see placement as career sampling or trial period for a job. Has unrealistic expectations – applies same criteria as he would for recruiting permanent staff.

Remedies:

- Improved employer briefing about objectives of placement, through briefing materials, personal contact by teacher, eg telephone or, better still, personal visit. Employer needs to be encouraged to see work experience as his opportunity to make a contribution to the personal development and education of young people, as a long-term investment in the young and in the community at large.
- Information given to employer about both student and school/college needs to be improved, eg leaflet about school, improved CV on pupil – including pupil's statement about what she hopes to get out of the placement, with the goal of gaining employer's sympathy and support.
- Pre-meeting between employer and student needs to be more structured so that employer understands student's needs better and is more supportive.

Case Study 5
Factors contributing to success:

- Student motivated to the extent that he is keen to do work experience – while his attendance and performance at school leave much to be desired.

Obstacles to success:

- Student inadequately briefed.
- Teacher's expectations of employer unrealistic and unreasonable – expects employer to have skills and inclination to take on teacher/disciplinarian role.

Remedies:

- Briefing of student inappropriate – may be better to suggest student looks for own placement – his not taking opportunity to do work experience is presented as *his* loss not teacher's.
- Better briefing of employer – be honest with him about student and explain potential difficulties – assure employer of school's willingness to support employer at first hint of trouble and encourage employer to seek that support.

Case Study 6
Factors contributing to success:

- Careful preparation of student.
- Parental support.
- Careful preparation of employer who is well informed and understanding.
- Staff at workplace are basically well meaning, caring and willing to make an effort for student.

Obstacles to success:

- Inadequate preparation of other staff in the workplace – lack of understanding of objectives of placement and of Fred's needs probably the cause of their impatience rather than lack of sympathy or willingness to support him.

Remedies:

- Ideally, teacher attends day centre staff meeting to discuss placement or talks informally to staff during the course of a pre-visit to placement.
- Superintendent be asked to do the same, perhaps supported by student CV or brief notes explaining the objectives of placement which she can give to staff.
- Fred to be put under the wing of an 'auntie' figure – a member of staff who takes particular responsibility for him and to whom Fred can turn. Superintendent needs to view such a role as a good experience of supervisory responsibility for the member of staff concerned and ensure that it is recognised as a positive feature of staff's own CV.

Case Study 7
Factors contributing to success:

- Motivated student.
- Caring, supportive employer – willing to take time to contact teacher and be flexible as far as possible in workplace arrangements; listens and makes constructive suggestions for remedying grievances.

Obstacles to success:

- Teacher and student ill-informed about hairdressing business.
- Student inadequately prepared, specifically on how to deal with problems and grievances – does not discuss them – just walks out.
- Monitoring inadequate – should have picked up problems earlier.

Remedies.

- Improved, more structured pre-placement meeting between employer and student – range of activities available might have been better covered and student's expectations better covered. See Chapter 3, specifically the interview *aide-mémoire* (Appendix 3.13, page 71) and employer's notes for guidance (Appendix 3.2, page 56).
- Advice of Careers Officer might have been helpful here.
- Improved preparation of student in dealing with problems constructively, see interview *aide-mémoire* (Appendix 3.13), last paragraph, and also role plays (Appendix 3.15, page 75).
- Improved monitoring practice – an early phone call might have picked up problems sooner.

Case Study 8

Factors contributing to success:

- Motivated student.
- Employer (Mike) committed and willing to make an effort.

Obstacles to success:

- Inadequate preparation of student – does not understand importance of time-keeping and the effect of his lateness on others.
- Other staff in the workplace not adequately briefed – Bill does not understand Andreas's need for a structured day and closer supervision – does not appreciate how important this placement is to Andreas and that Andreas – in spite of poor time-keeping – is genuinely keen.
- Student's domestic circumstances not taken fully into account. Likely that student is working until late in the evening at a physically exhausting job, in family business. This – on top of the longer hours of the placement and physical nature of work experience – is demanding.

Remedies:

- Better communication with Bill – who may be more sympathetic and patient if he understands Andreas's situation and how important the placement is to him. A more structured and planned pre-placement meeting, together with fuller information given to the employer about the student might have forestalled some of the problems. Also measures to ensure that this is effectively communicated to other staff with whom student will be working.

- Improved parental involvement – seek parent's support of son's career ambitions – possible lightening of student's workload in family business during period of placement.
- Better pre-placement preparation of student – this might have brought Andreas's circumstances to light. Also see Appendix 3.14, page 73, on time-keeping.
- Improved monitoring practice. A phone call early on in the placement might have picked up on potential difficulties sooner.

Case Study 9
Factors contributing to success:

- Sympathetic employer, genuinely trying to help Meena.

Obstacles to success:

- Inadequate briefing of employer – does not understand Meena's needs or ability level – his attempts to make the placement more varied and interesting for her are in fact overstretching her. His attempt to make her feel welcome by introducing her to lots of people is in fact overwhelming her.

Remedies:

- Better, more accurate information given to employer about student's level of ability, and needs for a slower pace and more protective environment.

Appendix II
The Health and Safety at Work Act 1974 – a summary

Duties of employers in respect of employees

1   The employer is obliged to provide and maintain *plant and systems of work* that are so far as is reasonably practicable, safe and without risks to health.
2   Every employer must make arrangements for ensuring, so far as is reasonably practicable, safety and absence of risks to health in connection with the *use, handling, storage and transport* of articles and substances.
3   The employer is obliged to provide such *information, instruction, training and supervision* as is necessary to ensure, so far as is reasonably practicable, the health and safety at work of his/her employees.
4   The employer must ensure safe access to and egress from places of work.
5   The employer is obliged to maintain a *working environment* which is, so far as is reasonably practicable, safe and without risks to health and adequate as regards facilities and arrangements for his/her employees' welfare at work.

Duties of employees

1   Every employee must take reasonable care for the health and safety of him/herself and of other persons who may be affected by his/her *acts or omissions* at work.
2   He/she must *cooperate with his/her employer* so far as is necessary to perform any duty or comply with any requirement imposed as a result of any law which may be in force.
3   He/she must *not interfere with or misuse* anything provided in the interest of health and safety.

Appendix III

Education (Work Experience) Act 1973

Chapter 23

An Act to enable education authorities to arrange for children under school-leaving age to have work experience, as part of their education.

[23 May 1973]

B e it enacted by the Queen's most Excellent Majesty, by and with the advice and consent of the Lords Spiritual and Temporal, and Commons, in this present Parliament assembled, and by the authority of the same, as follows:—

1.—(1) Subject to subsection (2) below, the enactments relating to the prohibition or regulation of the employment of children shall not apply to the employment of a child in his last year of compulsory schooling where the employment is in pursuance of arrangements made or approved by the local education authority or, in Scotland, the education authority with a view to providing him with work experience as part of his education.

Work experience in last year of compulsory schooling.

(2) Subsection (1) above shall not be taken to permit the employment of any person in any way contrary to—

    (*a*) an enactment which in terms applies to persons of less

than, or not over, a specified age expressed as a number
of years; or

(b) section 1(2) of the Employment of Women, Young
Persons and Children Act 1920 or (when it comes into
force) section 51(1) of the Merchant Shipping Act 1970
(prohibition of employment of children in ships);

1920 c. 65.

1970 c. 36.

(3) No arrangements shall be made under subsection (1) above
for a child to be employed in any way which would be contrary to
an enactment prohibiting or regulating the employment of young
persons if he were a young person (within the meaning of that
enactment) and not a child; and where a child is employed in
pursuance of arrangements so made, then so much of any
enactment as regulates the employment of young persons
(whether by excluding them from any description of work, or
prescribing the conditions under which they may be permitted to
do it, or otherwise howsoever) and would apply in relation to him
if he were of an age to be treated as a young person for the
purposes of that enactment shall apply in relation to him, in and
in respect of the employment arranged for him, in all respects as
if he were of an age to be so treated.

(4) In this Act—

'enactment' includes any byelaw, regulation or other provision
having effect under an enactment;

other expressions which are also used in the Education Acts
shall have the same meaning in this section as in those Acts;
and

'the Education Acts' means in England and Wales the Education
Acts 1944 to 1973 and, in Scotland, the Education (Scotland)
Acts 1939 to 1971;

and for the purposes of subsection (1) above a child is in his last
year of compulsory schooling at any time during the period of
twelve months before he attains the upper limit of compulsory
school age or, in Scotland, school age.

2.—(1) This Act may be cited as the Education (Work Experience) Act 1973; and—

(a) in relation to England and Wales, this Act shall be
included among the Acts which may be cited together as
the Education Acts 1944 to 1973; and

Citation and
extent.

(b) in relation to Scotland the Education Acts and this Act may be cited together as the Education (Scotland) Acts 1939 to 1973.

(2) Nothing in this Act extends to Northern Ireland.

EMPLOYMENT ACT 1990, CHAPTER 38

14. In section 1 of the Education (Work Experience) Act 1973 (work experience in the last year of compulsory schooling), in subsection (4) for the words from "a child is in his last year of compulsory schooling" to the end substitute "a child shall be taken to be in his last year of compulsory schooling from the beginning of the term at his school which precedes the beginning of the school year in which by virtue of section 9 of the Education Act 1962 he would be entitled to leave school.".

Period during which children may be employed for work experience. 1973 c. 23.